WONDERS OF CHEMISTRY

WONDERS OF CHEMISTRY

by

Archie Frederick Collins

YESTERDAY'S CLASSICS

ITHACA, NEW YORK

Cover and arrangement © 2018 Yesterday's Classics, LLC.

This edition, first published in 2018 by Yesterday's Classics, an imprint of Yesterday's Classics, LLC, is an unabridged republication of the text originally published by Thomas Y. Crowell Company in 1922. For the complete listing of the books that are published by Yesterday's Classics, please visit www.yesterdaysclassics.com. Yesterday's Classics is the publishing arm of the Baldwin Online Children's Literature Project which presents the complete text of hundreds of classic books for children at www.mainlesson.com.

ISBN: 978-1-63334-104-3

Yesterday's Classics, LLC
PO Box 339
Ithaca, NY 14851

PREFACE

Chemistry is a closed book to many of us. We regard it as something difficult, hard to understand, and remote, when as a matter of fact it is inherently one of the most interesting of subjects. Instead of being remote, it is part and parcel of our daily lives. It sums up the whole process of nature. Each one of our every-day habits—eating, drinking, breathing—is nothing more nor less than a chemical reaction.

The recent World War brought us to a sharp realization of just what chemistry may mean for us in the future, either for weal or woe. On the one hand it produced insidious gases, powerful explosives and the deadliest agents of destruction that the world ever witnessed. On the other, it came to the aid of more than one nation by supplying nitrates for the soil and artificial clothing and foodstuffs.

To make us acquainted with some of the wonders of every-day chemistry is the purpose of this book. It is not concerned with the scientific side except incidentally. The author is a practical experimenter who knows whereof he speaks, and better still knows how to tell the reader about it in understandable language. He takes us behind the scenes, as it were, and points out the marvellous little elves called "atoms" actually at work. He presupposes no advance knowledge as he takes the reader on this fascinating trip through his laboratory. He first discusses the wonders of air and water, and that modern magic, liquid air. Then he takes up common acids and salts, metals and alloys, gases, explosives, and other topics of live interest. We learn something of the magic of coal tar, from which the most beautiful colors and delicate flavors are obtained. There are talks on photography, artificial diamonds, radium, and the electric blast furnace with its heat running into the thousands of degrees.

These are but a few of the marvels of chemistry, which are fascinating on their own account, and are also of tremendous importance to each one of us. While primarily addressed to young folks, this book has a message to older readers as well.

CONTENTS

I. The Wonders of Air.............1
II. The Marvels of Water..........14
III. Fire, Heat, and Fuel..............26
IV. Some Useful Acids..............40
V. Old Metals and New Alloys....52
VI. Gases, Good and Bad...........65
VII. From Gunpowder to TNT.......76
VIII. How Plants Live and Grow.....88
IX. Chemistry of Every-Day Things......................101
X. Cellulose and Other Fibers...113
XI. Colors, Pigments, and Paints..127
XII. Chemistry of the Sunbeam.....139
XIII. Electro-Chemical Processes..152
XIV. Products of Synthetic Chemistry......................166

XV. THE MAGIC OF COAL-TAR 177

XVI. MAKING PERFUMES AND
      FLAVORS 189

XVII. ELECTRIC FURNACE PRODUCTS.... 199

XVIII. SYNTHETIC DIAMONDS AND
      OTHER GEMS 212

XIX. RADIUM, THE MODERN MARVEL... 225

XX. THE COMING MIRACLES OF
      CHEMISTRY.................... 237

CHAPTER I

THE WONDERS OF AIR

IF you will go out into the open on a clear night and find the *North Star* and then look around a little you will see the constellation of the *Big Dipper* on one side of it and the constellation of *Cassiopeia*, which is formed like the letter *W*, on the other side of it. Now draw an imaginary line through the middle of the Big Dipper, the North Star and Cassiopeia and let it project beyond the latter when it will pass through a hazy patch of light, and this is the *Great Nebula of Andromeda.*

Where Our Atmosphere Came From.—On looking at this nebula through a powerful telescope you would instantly see that it is not made up of myriads of stars but of something that seems very much like fog, or vapor, or smoke, with a bright spot in its center and other and smaller bright spots scattered through it here and there, and these have quite a solid appearance. It was from just such a nebula as this that our *solar system* was made, our *sun* being formed of the bright central part, and our *earth* and the other planets growing from the smaller bright parts. This nebula contained all of the gases and other elements which go to make up the earth, together with its envelope of air.

How the Atmosphere Behaves.—The atmosphere, as the air surrounding the earth is called, is often likened to a great ocean, the lower part resting on the surface of it just as water does, and it stays there for the same reason, and that is because it has weight. While a little air has no appreciable weight, the atmosphere reaches upward to a height of from fifty to two hundred miles and the amount of it is enough to make it press on the surface of the earth, at sea level, with a weight of nearly fifteen pounds to the square inch. This pressure is always changing a little, as some parts of it become heated more than others, and in equalizing the temperature the air is put into motion, and in this way the *winds* are set up.

What the Atmosphere is Made Of.—While you cannot sense the air when it is perfectly still, you can *feel* it when it is moving, that is when a breeze, or the wind, is blowing, and you can then also *hear* the effects of it. Air is formed chiefly of two gases, *oxygen* and *nitrogen*, in the proportion of one part of the former to four parts of the latter.

These very unlike gases, however, are merely mixed together and not combined chemically; indeed if they were combined they would not form air but one of the *oxides* of *nitrogen*. The Chinese knew that air contained an active element, which is the oxygen in it, away back in the eighth century. They also knew that it would combine with sulphur, charcoal and some metals, and how to obtain it from saltpetre. The first person, however, to show that the air was formed of two gases was Leonardo da Vinci, who lived during the last half of the fifteenth century. But it was away along in the eighteenth century before the first pure sample of oxygen was made by Joseph Priestley, and this he did by heating *mercuric oxide*. He called the gas so obtained *dephlogisticated air*,[1] and a few years later the name *oxygen*[2] was given to it by Lavoisier, the greatest chemist of his time.

Nitrogen, the other chief gas of the air, was discovered by Rutherford, of Edinburgh, a couple of years before Priestley found a way to obtain oxygen. His experiment consisted of shutting up an animal in an air-tight compartment; he then removed the *carbon dioxide*, which was given off when the animal breathed, by absorbing it with charcoal, when he found that a gas still remained which would not support life.

But the fact that nitrogen existed in the air as a separate gas was first shown by Lavoisier. He called it *azote*, which means *without life*, and the French still use this name for it. We get the word *nitrogen* from the Latin *nitrum*, which means *saltpetre*. The oxygen of the air, then, is the gas that supports and sustains life, and the nitrogen simply serves to dilute and spread it about.

[1] In Priestley's day (1750) *phlogiston* was the name given to a supposed principle that was thought to be a necessary part of every substance which burns. Thus when he heated mercuric oxide he assumed that the phlogiston had been separated from the gas (oxygen) which remained, and hence he called the latter *dephlogisticated* air. It was Lavoisier who overthrew the phlogiston theory.

[2] The word oxygen means acid former, and Lavoisier believed that oxygen was the one essential constituent needed to form an acid. Later it was found to be nitrogen and not oxygen.

Other Substances in the Air.—Carbon Dioxide.—
Here are two easy experiments which you should make. *First*, take a glass of *lime water* which is a clear and colorless solution, and blow through a straw into it when it will become milky white. *Second*, light a piece of candle and let it down into a bottle which has a little lime water in it; you will not have long to wait until a white crust will begin to form on it. These experiments show very clearly that not only your breath and the candle give off some kind of a gas but that the gas in each case is the same. This gas is often called *carbonic acid gas*, but its right name is *carbon dioxide*.

There is not very much carbon dioxide in the air compared with the oxygen and nitrogen, and it varies in different localities. In cities where fuels are burned the amount of it is in the neighborhood of six parts to 10,000 parts of air, while in the country there are only about three parts in 10,000 parts of air. The amount is kept pretty constant, for while growing vegetation absorbs large quantities of it, this is replaced all the time by animals which exhale it, burning fuels, decaying meats and vegetable matter and fermentation in wines, and in various other substances which keep giving it off.

The *choke-damp* of the miners is really carbon dioxide, and while it is not poisonous it will not support life; this is the reason why deaths often result when men in mines have to breathe too much of it. The human body, though, can stand a considerable amount of carbon dioxide above the usual three or six per cent. without causing death or even producing any untoward result, as is shown in works where it is made for charging mineral and soda waters.

Water Vapor.—Another substance that is always found in the air, however dry it may seem to be, is *water vapor*. When you step out of doors on a cold day you can see the water vapor that is in your warm breath every time you exhale it into the colder air. The amount of water vapor that the air can hold depends on the temperature of the latter. When the air contains as much water vapor as it can hold it is then said to be *saturated*, and hot air can be saturated with more water vapor than cold air.

The reason you can see your breath when you exhale it into cold air is because the warm air which you exhale is not saturated with water vapor, but as your breath strikes the cold air the latter is saturated with it, which makes it visible. This also explains why moisture collects on a tumbler of cold water when it is placed in a warm room and frost forms on a window pane when it is warm inside and cold outside. Since cold air has less power to hold water vapor than warm air, as the warm moisture-laden air begins to cool off in the night, the water vapor condenses into water and clings to the grass and other objects, and this is what we call *dew*.

When there is a thick fog or it begins to rain, it is because the atmosphere is saturated with water vapor. The amount of water vapor in the atmosphere determines its *humidity*, and when the saturation point is nearly reached, that is when the humidity is high, the pores of our bodies cannot throw off the excess water by evaporation and so we feel oppressed. And the reverse is also true, for when there is very little water vapor in the air, that is when the humidity is low, we perspire too freely and this, too, is unpleasant. Where hot air or steam is used to heat a room it tends to dry out the moisture in the air; this can be compensated for by placing a pan of water on the radiator or near the register so that the evaporation will make up for that which is lost.

Dust and Germs.—The air at all times contains dust of many varieties and germs of many kinds. When you are in a theatre and a *spotlight* is thrown from the gallery onto the stage you will see the course of the beam of light, but this is only because the light is reflected by the dust particles in its path,—for a beam of light itself cannot be seen.

What we call dust is not made up of particles of dry matter alone, but frequently it contains millions of germs; that is, minute animals that are alive and kicking and which have the power, many of them, to produce disease unless our bodies are in such an excellent state of health as to be able to ward off their attacks. These germs for the most part are formed of single cells, and when we take them into our bodies where it is nice and warm and they have plenty of water and lots of good food, they start in to multiply at a great rate. Then there are yeasts that make wines ferment, and those of still another kind that cause meats and vegetables to decay. So you see there are good little germs as well as bad little germs.

Nitric Acid, Ammonia and Ozone.—Besides the chief gases which make up the atmosphere other substances are found in it which are very useful to us. The first of these is *nitric acid*, and this is the way it is formed in the upper layers of air: Whenever a flash of lightning takes place, the heat of it causes the oxygen and nitrogen to combine, and this produces the oxides of nitrogen; in turn these combine with the water vapor that is in the air, and the result is *nitric acid*. How nitric acid is extracted by electricity from the air and the many uses of it will be explained in a chapter further on.

There is also a very small amount of *ammonia* in the atmosphere and its presence there is due to decaying vegetable and animal matter which gives it off; it is then distributed through the air by diffusion. When there is enough of it in the air it is dissolved by the water vapor and later when it rains it is carried to the soil. There it is converted into compounds of ammonium and these are finally changed into nitric acid, which is a good food for the soil.

Ozone is a condensed form of oxygen, having three atoms of oxygen to a molecule instead of one, and this makes them act quite differently from one another. When an electric spark passes through the air it changes the oxygen into ozone, and so when there is an electric storm ozone is produced and some think that they can detect its presence by the peculiar refreshing odor, which is rather due to the cleanness of the air.

Recently Discovered Gases of the Air.—In 1894, Lord Rayleigh and Sir William Ramsay, British scientists

THE MARVELS OF LIQUID AIR

(a) In the glass jar experiment, liquid air first floats, then the oxygen sinks in bubbles, as the nitrogen boils. (b) Mercury is frozen solid into a hammer. (c) A teakettle containing liquid air boils when placed on a cake of ice.

of renown, discovered that the atmosphere contained traces of a new gas which they called *argon*. The way they came to make the discovery was like this: They had obtained some nitrogen from the air by removing the oxygen, when they found that it was heavier than the nitrogen they had made by decomposing an ammonia compound called ammonium nitrite.

After many experiments they came to the conclusion that there must be some other substance in the air which made the nitrogen heavier than that which they obtained from other substances, and this they discovered to be a gas. They called this gas *argon* from two Greek words which mean *inactive*, as all attempts thus far to make it combine with other elements have proved unsuccessful.

Sir William Ramsay discovered three new gases in the atmosphere in 1898, when it became possible to make liquid air on a large scale, and these are *neon*, *xenon*, and *krypton*. Neon, named from the Greek word which means new, was separated from the air by letting a quart or so of liquid air evaporate. As the lighter gases passed off first, the heavier gases, of which *neon* is one, remained at the bottom of the container. It was shown by Ramsay that there is one part of neon in 100,000 parts of air.

The gas xenon, which means *stranger*, is another inactive chemical element that is left after the other gases have evaporated from liquid air. It is the heaviest of all the gases found in the air. Krypton, which means *hidden*, is another of the rare gases which Ramsay discovered in the air, and it has a density of about twice that of argon. It exists in the proportion of about one part to a million parts of air.

How Air Supports Life.—If the air supply is cut off from an animal it will quickly die of suffocation. As you know, man and all the more highly developed animals breathe by means of lungs and in doing so they take the oxygen from the air. It is the oxygen that supports life and after it is received into the lungs it is absorbed by the blood and carried to every part of the body.

Now the cells of animals are made up very largely of carbon and hydrogen, and when the oxygen in the blood comes in contact with them they combine and produce two different compounds; that is, the oxygen which combines with the carbon of the cells produces *carbon dioxide*, and the oxygen which combines with the hydrogen produces *water*. The carbon dioxide is carried back by the blood to the lungs of the animal, where it is exhaled into the air, while the water is carried off by the kidneys, the lungs and the skin.

Plants breathe as well as animals, but they do this through little openings, called *stomata*, on the under side of their leaves. But, different from animals, plants inhale the carbon dioxide that is in the air, and this is where the carbon comes from, of which they are so largely formed. The carbon dioxide also combines with some of the water that the roots have absorbed and this forms *sugar*, *starch* and *cellulose*, which latter is the woody fibers of the plant. On combining with the water some oxygen is set free and this goes back into the air. From this cycle of operations you will see that there is a constant balance maintained between the oxygen that animals take out of the air and the plants take in, and the carbon dioxide that the plants take out of it and the animals exhale.

Experiments With Liquid Air.—How Liquid Air is Made.—In 1895, Linde, a Swedish chemist, discovered a process by which very low temperatures could be obtained—temperatures as low, nearly, as minus 200 degrees—and this method has since been used for the production of *liquid air*. This process consists of compressing ordinary air and taking the heat out of it by making it flow through pipes immersed in cold water. When the compressed air is cool it is allowed to escape through a nozzle when the air expands, and this again very greatly lowers its temperature.

The chilled stream of air is next made to flow around the pipe which carries the air after it is cooled with water and before it escapes through the nozzle, and this process is repeated so that each time a lower temperature is had until finally a point is reached at which the air becomes a liquid. This is the process that is now in general use for liquefying air and other gases.

The Apparatus Used.—The apparatus of a liquid air plant is generally made up of a two-stage air compressor, that is a compressor having two cylinders, a low pressure and a high pressure one, and this is driven by steam or electric power. The air which is to be liquefied has the water vapor and carbon dioxide extracted from it when

APPARATUS FOR MAKING LIQUID AIR

it is admitted into the first cylinder of the compressor, where it is compressed to about 200 pounds to the square inch.

The air under this pressure then flows through a coil of pipe immersed in cold water, and when it is thoroughly cooled it is allowed to flow through a small nozzle into the second cylinder of the compressor, where it is compressed to 2,000 pounds to the square inch. It is again made to flow through a coil of pipe and is cooled to a still lower temperature by the air which has previously been compressed and cooled, and this changes it into a liquid.

About Liquid Air.—The liquid air thus produced has a pale, sky-blue color, and if allowed to flow out on a plate or into a common bottle it will instantly commence to boil, as ordinary air is so much hotter than it is, and it will continue to boil until all of it has evaporated into the air again. How to keep liquid air after having obtained it was a great problem to the scientists for a while, but Sir James Dewar solved it by inventing a bottle with a double wall—a bottle within a bottle—and then pumping the air out of the space between them. This construction insulates the inside bottle from the outside one so that it takes a long time for the heat of the air outside to penetrate through the vacuum and reach it. This is the origin of the *thermos bottle* which is now so popular for keeping hot liquids hot and cold liquids cold.

Experiments With Liquid Air.—If you have a quart or so of liquid air you can perform magical marvels the

THE WONDERS OF AIR

like of which the old and honored tribe of Hindu *fakirs* never dreamed. Among these is freezing some mercury into the shape of a hammer; when it sets to a solid it looks very much like silver, and you can use it to drive nails. Drop a hollow rubber ball into a glass of liquid air and when it is frozen it becomes as brittle as though it were made of glass; now throw it on the floor and it will break into a hundred pieces. A beefsteak when frozen in liquid air will ring out like a gong if you strike it with a hammer, but you must not strike it too hard or it will fly to pieces. These are just a few of the many startling experiments that you can make with liquid air, and what it may lead to in the future no one knows.

CHAPTER II

THE MARVELS OF WATER

When the world was in the making there were terrific lightning storms and these great electrical discharges, together with the heat generated by the mighty upheavals of primordial matter, caused the hydrogen and the oxygen to combine chemically as *water vapor* in the atmosphere. This vapor finally fell as liquid water and blanketed the earth and this was the origin of the lakes, seas, and rivers.

What Water Is.—Different from the air, which is a mere mechanical mixture of its two constituent gases, water is formed of free oxygen and free hydrogen in the proportion of one part of the former and two parts of the latter by volume, that is by bulk. Now, these gases will not combine at ordinary temperatures, neither will they burn when they are combined. This, obviously, is a very wise provision, for so inflammable are each of these gases separately that a mere spark would suffice to ignite them, and so fire the whole world.

When oxygen and hydrogen are merely mixed together, like the nitrogen and oxygen of the air, they are very explosive, and when they explode they combine chemically, the resultant product of which is the liquid we call *water*. If a jet of hydrogen is burned in a jet of oxygen they will not explode provided the correct proportions of each gas are maintained. Under these conditions the flame thus produced is, with the exception of the electric arc, the hottest that we know how to make. To obtain the oxy-hydrogen flame a special nozzle is used, and when the flame is directed on a piece of lime it heats it to incandescence and this makes a dazzling light. This *oxy-hydrogen* light, as it is called, was used for years in stereopticons and for spotlights in theatres before the electric light displaced it.

There are two laboratory experiments you can make which prove that water is really formed of oxygen and hydrogen. One of these is to decompose it with a current of electricity, and the other is to combine the two gases by igniting them with an electric spark. To decompose water is easy, for you need only to invert two test-tubes filled with water in a tumbler of water and bring one end of one of the wires of an electric battery under and into one test-tube, and the other wire from the battery under and into the other test-tube. (See Chapter XIII.)

Water that is ordinarily pure will not conduct an electric current, and to make it do so you must put a few drops of sulphuric acid into it. This done, switch on the current and you will see a lot of little bubbles form on each of the ends of the wires, or *electrodes*, and, presently, you will also observe that the water in the upper ends of the tubes is falling, and, moreover, that it falls twice as fast in one tube as it does in the other. This is because the spaces in the tubes are being filled with gases which displace the water as it is formed and that twice as much hydrogen is being formed as oxygen.

As these gases have no color you cannot see them and so to know they are actually there and to tell them apart you must make some kind of a test. This you can do by removing the tube, closed end up, in which there is the least water and holding a lighted match to the mouth of it. There will be a miniature explosion, which is the proof that it contains hydrogen gas and it will burn with a flame that is just about the color of air. To test the other tube for oxygen, remove the tube, closed end up, light a match and blow out the flame of it so that only a kindling spark remains; push it into the tube when it will instantly burst into a flame again, and this proves that it contains oxygen.

Further tests will show that the sulphuric acid added to the water to make it a conductor remains after the water has been *electrolyzed*, as it is called. While the above experiment proves that oxygen and hydrogen have been separated out from the water it does not prove that water is formed of them and nothing else. To show this conclusively you need a laboratory apparatus called a *eudiometer;* this consists of a graduated tube so that two volumes of hydrogen and one volume of oxygen can be passed into it. In the upper end of the tube, which is closed, a pair of platinum wires is sealed in so that a small spark-gap is formed.

Now as long as the hydrogen and the oxygen in the tube are not subjected to heat they will remain

THE MARVELS OF WATER

merely mixed, but the instant that an electric spark is made to jump across the spark-gap the two gases will explode and chemically combine when a minute drop of water will be produced. Since it takes more than 2,000 volumes of the mixed gases to make one volume of water it is easy to see why the resultant amount of the latter is so very small.

How Water Behaves.—Water in its pure state has neither taste nor odor. If you will hold a glass of it between your eyes and a source of light it will appear to be without color, but if you look at a large quantity of it as, for instance, a lake, it takes on a blue color. This is often supposed to be due to the reflection of the sky, but, as a matter of fact, it is the natural color of the water itself when it is pure or nearly so.

There are three states that water can take on and these are (1) *liquid*, (2) *steam*, and (3) *ice*. At all temperatures between 212 degrees above zero and 32 degrees above zero, using a *Fahrenheit*[3] thermometer, water remains a liquid. When it is heated to 212 degrees it boils at sea-level, and oppositely when it is cooled to 32 degrees it freezes.

When water boils it is converted into true steam, and this is a vapor that cannot be seen. When this vapor passes into the colder air it condenses into minute drops of water. An easy experiment to show that true steam cannot be seen is to take a flask, such as chemists use,

---

[3]Fahrenheit, a German physicist, who lived 1686–1736, invented the mercurial thermometer, and made the scale that gives the boiling point of water at 212 degrees and the freezing point at 32 degrees.

partly fill it with water and heat it over the flame of an alcohol lamp or a Bunsen burner. When it boils you will know that steam is being generated and yet you cannot see it in the space above the water. The moment you uncork the flask, though, you will see the so-called steam rising from it in the air.

It is well known that all metals, except certain alloys, and many other solid substances, when heated and which are then allowed to cool, contract; that is they shrink a little. Water, when cooled, likewise shrinks until it reaches a temperature of plus 39 degrees, Fahrenheit, which is seven degrees above its freezing-point. Water is then the heavier. As the temperature falls from 39° to 32° it expands, and the colder water (32°) is at the top of the vessel, as it begins to solidify, that is, to change into ice.

Since the density of ice is less than water it weighs proportionately less, and this is the reason why ice forms on the surface of water as well as floats on top of it. If water continued to shrink as it became ice it would sink and choke up the waterways and besides it might never melt. The mighty force set up by water when it begins to freeze is a phenomenon that you are probably well acquainted with, for it is then that it bursts water-pipes, cracks milk bottles and plays havoc in general. At the end of this chapter we shall tell you how artificial ice is manufactured.

Kinds and Uses of Water.—There is, of course, only one kind of water chemically, but physically there are many different kinds depending on whether it is impure or pure, that is, contains foreign substances or not. Pure water, as you have seen, consists of hydrogen and oxygen and contains nothing else, and this may be obtained in quantities by distilling ordinary water. Rain water is, generally speaking, as free from impurities as is ever found in nature, but as it always contains other substances, it cannot be really called pure. Well and spring water that look so clear and sparkling contain mineral substances of various kinds, while surface water fairly teems with germs, some of which are harmless, while others produce virulent diseases.

Water is the natural drink of man, but as he grew in curiosity and knowledge he experimented with its effect on other substances and so found among other things, that certain herbs, fruit and grains when steeped, boiled and distilled with water produced drinks that were pleasing to the taste and stimulating to the system. Water, however, is necessary to the well-being of all living things, since they themselves, whether plants or animals, are formed of three-fourths part of it. Hence the matter of providing a supply that is free from harmful substances is a vital one to the human race.

And this is also true in the arts and industries, for many kinds of water contain substances which make them unsuitable for certain purposes and, what is more to the point, they are actually injurious, as you will presently see.

About Drinking Water.—Drinking water, or *potable water* as it is called, plays a large part in determining the state of the health, and, consequently, it is important that it should be of the right kind. Now, as already stated, water from springs and deep wells is generally free from germs, but it always contains more or less mineral matter. As the water soaks through the soil the germs in it become attached to the particles of the latter and are not carried down with it; on the other hand, as the water comes in contact with the minerals of the soil it dissolves some of them and carries them along in solution.

If a well is dug, a pump is driven, or the stream finds its way to the surface, as a spring, the water will be pure and wholesome because the disease germs have been filtered out of it. Should the underground stream reach the sea, it carries the mineral substances with it, and when the sea water evaporates, only pure water goes up and, this comes down again as rain.

You can easily find out the amount of foreign matter there is in any kind of water, for all you need to do is to fill a porcelain dish with some of it and heat it over an alcohol, or a Bunsen, flame until it has all evaporated, when the solid matter will remain behind. Where the water seeps through soil containing granite rock very little of the latter will be dissolved away, but where the water comes in contact with limestone large amounts of the latter will be dissolved.

Soft and Hard Water.—Rain water and other kinds of water that contain very little mineral matter are called *soft water*, while, oppositely, water that contains limestone and other mineral substances is called *hard water*. As a matter of fact, water of any kind that contains enough mineral matter to make soap curdle is hard water. Where there are more than twenty-five parts of mineral matter in a million parts of water it does not affect it to the extent of making it hard, but where there are more than fifty parts of mineral matter in a million parts of water it makes it quite hard.

There are two kinds of hard water, and these are: (1) *temporary* hard water, and (2) *permanent* hard water. The difference between them is that you can get rid of the hardness of the first kind by boiling it, since it contains limestone, and this is precipitated, that is, it is thrown down, and deposited on the inside of the kettle. But boiling will not remove the hardness of the second kind for the reason that it contains *gypsum*, or, rather, calcium sulphate, which cannot be precipitated in this way. You can, however, soften permanent hard water to some extent by adding *sal soda* to it, as this tends to precipitate the gypsum when sodium sulphate is left in solution.

How Soap Acts on Water.—When you put soap into soft water it makes it lather or suds, because there is little or no mineral matter in it. But when you put soap into hard water it combines with the mineral substances chemically and forms a compound that cannot be dissolved. If, however, you precipitate the limestone that is in hard water by boiling, or the gypsum by adding sal soda to it as described above, the soap and water will then lather or suds freely.

Where hard water is the only kind available for use in the home it becomes quite an item of expense for it wastes the soap in proportion to its hardness. Not only this, but where it is very hard, the mineral substances get into the pores of the skin and the soap will have very little effect in getting them out. So, too, they lodge between the meshes of goods that are washed and in the same way and for the same reason it is quite impossible to get them clean. Nearly all laundry soaps and washing powders have an excess of soda in them to soften hard water and this has a very bad effect on the goods.

Boiler Water and Boiler Scale.—If you will look into a teakettle you will see, if you use well water in it, that the inside of it is incrusted, or has *fur* on it, as it is sometimes called. This is, of course, the precipitate of the mineral matter caused by boiling the water. Where hard water is used for running engines and steam plants the same action takes place, though on a larger scale and with a more destructive effect. That is to say, the inside of the boiler and tubes becomes coated with the mineral matter and this prevents the heat from passing through them and wastes the coal. There are other disadvantages in using hard water in boilers, and among them are: (1) the boiler scale and boiler plate, of which the boiler is made, expand at different rates and this often leads to weakening the seams; (2) the scale may cause the tubes to get red-hot and this not only shortens the life of the boiler but may cause it to explode; (3) it pits the tubes of the boiler, and (4) it causes the water to foam.

The easiest and cheapest method of keeping a boiler from scaling and pitting and the water from foaming is to use soft water, but this is not always practical. The next best thing is to get rid of the hardness of the water if hard water must be used. If the hardness is temporary the water can be boiled before it is used in the boiler or it can be treated by adding *milk of lime* which is made by stirring slaked lime in water.

To soften boiler water whose hardness is permanent, lime water is added to it, but the amount used must be according to the amount of mineral matter there is in it. Where boiler water has both limestone and gypsum in it so that it has both temporary and permanent hardness, both can be removed by adding a solution of crude caustic soda to it. What is called the *permutit process* is also widely used for softening boiler water. Permutit is a coarse kind of sand, and when the water to be used is filtered through it the mineral substances react with the sand, and the sodium, which is in the sand, replaces the calcium in the water. The sodium compound goes into the boiler with the water but has no action except to clean it.

Purifying Water on a Big Scale.—To provide water in sufficient quantities to supply cities has been one of the great problems of civilized mankind, but it is only during the last fifty years or so that the necessity for purifying water for drinking purposes has been fully taken into account. Now there are several ways by which water can be purified and among the more important are by: (1) *boiling*, (2) *aeration*, (3) *chemical processes*, (4) the *ozone process*, (5) *biological processes*, (6) the *coagulation method*, and (7) *mechanical separation*.

For purifying water on a small scale, as for home

use, boiling is the simplest and best method. But for purifying water on a large scale the last-named six methods given above are employed either separately or in combination. Aerating the water is done either by throwing it into the air or else letting it fall over a steep hill of rocks. In either case when the water comes into contact with the air some of the oxygen of the latter is dissolved out of it. While this treatment improves the water it does not purify it to any great extent.

One of the chemical processes consists of adding bleaching powder to the water, when chlorine is liberated and this gas kills off all the harmful germs. *Ozone*, which is a vigorous form of oxygen, is produced by electric discharges in the air and this when introduced into the water also kills off the germs. Ozone is far better than chlorine for this purpose, as an excess of the former in the water cannot be detected, whereas any excess of the latter gives the water a bad taste. The most curious of all methods for purifying water is that of putting germs that are harmless to the human system into the water and these kill off the harmful germs. This is known as a *biological process*.

Another curious way of ridding water of germs is by the *coagulation process*. In this process a harmless glue-like substance is put into the water, and the germs and other impurities stick to it. The mass is then separated out from the water when the latter is left comparatively pure. In the *sedimentation method* much of the impurities, including the germs, falls to the bottom, but it does not get rid of all of them. Usually after sedimentation the water is passed through mechanical or sand filters which remove the rest of the germs and other impurities.

How Artificial Ice is Made.—Making Ice With Ammonia.—Ammonia is one of the easiest gases to liquefy, and this property is taken advantage of in making artificial ice. To liquefy ammonia gas all that is necessary is to compress it, causing it to lose heat. Then, when the pressure is removed, the liquefied ammonia expands into a gas again and as it does so it absorbs a large amount of heat. In this latter operation the heat which it absorbs is taken from water which surrounds the ammonia pipes and this produces a freezing temperature.

The apparatus used for the manufacture of ice by the ammonia process consists of a compressor driven by an engine or other source of power, a water-cooled series of pipes, and a cooling-tank. Ammonia gas is passed into the compression cylinder where it is compressed and liquefied, then it is passed through a series of pipes on which cold water drips.

It is next allowed to expand into a gas, and as it does so it flows through another series of pipes immersed in a tank of *brine*, that is a solution of salt and water, which will not freeze at the temperature of ordinary water. As the ammonia flows through these pipes it absorbs the heat of the brine until the temperature of the latter drops to below plus 32 degrees Fahrenheit, which is the freezing-point of ordinary water. Sheet-steel cans filled with distilled water are immersed in the brine, and thus the water in them is frozen.

CHAPTER III

FIRE, HEAT, AND FUEL

To make and to use fire belongs to mankind alone. None of the animals, not even the manlike apes, such as the gibbon, orang and chimpanzee, know how to use fire, much less how to make it. But when the first man was evolved, something like a million years ago, his first real exploit that set him above the monkey family was to use fire. Then, with the coming of modern man, or *Homo-sapiens* (which means man-wise), came the knowledge of how to make a fire when and where he wanted it.

Origin of Ways of Making Fire.—It is easy to guess that before primitive man had learned how to make fire for himself he obtained it from the hot ashes, or lava, that was thrown out, or flowed down, into a valley from some volcano, or that he found a tree ablaze which the lightning had struck, or the dried grass burning where a meteor had fallen. As to the method he first employed to make a fire it seems reasonably certain that it was either by striking two stones together or by rubbing a stick of wood against another and softer piece.

The *concussion* method, as the first is called, was

carried on through the ages, with the slight modification of using a piece of steel in the place of one of the rocks, until the middle of the last century when matches came into general use. The first friction match was, however, invented as far back as the fifteenth century. Robert Boyle, who was one of the first of the real chemists, discovered, in 1680, how to obtain *phosphorus*, and under his direction Godfrey Hawkwitz made a match by dipping a wood splint in *sulphur* and then securing a bit of phosphorus to it.

The reason phosphorus is used is because it ignites at a very low temperature; in fact, *yellow phosphorus* will take fire when it is exposed to air, while *red phosphorus* must be heated a trifle before it will do so, and a little friction is all that is needed. Owing to the danger and trouble of using the phosphorus, which was evidently of the yellow kind, and also to its high cost, the match did not come into general use until more than one hundred and fifty years later.

What Fire and Flame Are.—When a substance combines violently with oxygen, which the air supplies in unlimited quantities, both heat and light are produced, and we say that the substance is *burning* while we call the phenomenon *fire*. The act or operation of something *burning* is called *combustion*, but burning and combustion are words that are generally used to mean the same thing. Many substances which burn contain hydrogen and other gases, and when these are ignited they stream forth into the air and produce *light*. In nearly all kinds of flame the light is set up by solid particles formed chiefly of carbon suspended in the gas and heated to incandescence—that is white hot.

Burning and the Kindling Point.—Before you can make a piece of paper or wood burn you must heat it, and until you have heated it to a certain degree of temperature it will not take fire. The lowest temperature at which paper, wood, or any other substance will ignite is called its *kindling point*, or *kindling temperature*, and this differs with different substances. That different substances have different kindling points is taken advantage of in making parlor matches; that is one end of the splint is dipped into melted paraffin and this is coated with a compound of phosphorus and chlorate of potassium.

Now when you strike the match the heat developed by the friction fires the phosphorus and frees the oxygen of the chlorate of potassium and in burning this heats the paraffin until its kindling point is reached and it takes fire; this in turn heats the wood splint until its kindling point is reached when it finally takes fire. That a substance must have its temperature raised to the kindling point before it can ignite is a wise precaution of nature, for if it did not prevail, the moment any kind of combustible material came into contact with oxygen it would take fire. Bear in mind that the kindling point of a substance is the *lowest* temperature at which it will ignite and that it has nothing to do with the temperature set up by the substance when it is burning.

When Things Burn in Air.—To make a substance burn, you must have plenty of oxygen present and raise the temperature of the substance to the kindling point. The oxygen that is in the air furnishes enough of this gas for all ordinary burning purposes and most materials that burn, especially those we use for fuel, are composed chiefly of carbon, hydrogen and such substances as will combine readily with oxygen when they are raised to the kindling point.

Temperatures that are very much higher than those when ordinary substances burn can be had by burning aluminum in oxygen which is set free from some of the oxides of metals such as *ferric oxide,* that is iron rust. The great affinity of aluminum for oxygen when it is fired makes it burn at a temperature high enough to melt any of the metals. This forms the basis of welding and producing pure metals known as the Goldschmidt *thermit process* and you will find more about it in the chapter on *metals*.

How to Start and Put Out a Fire.—To start a fire easily you must have an excess of oxygen and this is the reason why you use paper or shavings first, and kindling wood next before you put on the wood or coal. This is also why you fan the fire with your hat, blow on it with your mouth or, better, with a bellows blower. To keep the fuel burning after it takes fire there must be sufficient oxygen and hydrogen to combine fast enough to keep the temperature higher than the kindling point, and to set free the products of combustion.

The way to put out a fire is just the reverse of kindling and keeping it going. Where a fire has just started, a quick way to put it out is to smother it with a blanket as this keeps the oxygen away from it and the carbon dioxide around it. Where a building is burning water is thrown on it, as this takes up much of the heat by absorbing it, keeps the temperature below its kindling point, while the steam that is formed prevents the air from supplying more oxygen to it. Fire extinguishers are made so that when they are opened they will generate carbon dioxide, or some other vapor that will not burn or support combustion, and the pressure of these gases throws a stream of water on the blazing material.

About Spontaneous Combustion.—When oxygen combines with other substances whose temperature has been raised above the kindling point it oxidizes them and they either decay or rust. The chemical action is quite like burning but, of course, there is very little heat developed and usually no light is produced. When oxygen combines with some substances, as for instance linseed oil in which wool is soaked, the heat developed may not be released; if it is kept in by the wool until it becomes hot enough to raise the temperature to the kindling point, the material takes fire and this is called *spontaneous combustion.*

Heat is a Form of Energy.—Heat is a form of energy and not a form of matter as it was once thought to be. Heat can be produced in different ways, as for instance by friction, by passing a current through a wire which has resistance, and by chemical action. The latter method is the one that we are interested in here as a means of producing heat. Now all substances of whatever kind are made up of little particles of matter called *atoms*, and when a substance is burning, the action of the carbon and hydrogen atoms in combining with the oxygen gives rise to vibrations in the ether which permeates and surrounds all matter. It is by these vibrations in the ether that the light and heat are transmitted from the burning body. If the vibrations of the ether come into contact with your body they act on the *thermal nerves* of it and in this way you get the sensation of heat.

Heat as a Power Producer.—There are different ways by which power can be produced as, for instance, by using the wind, the water and heat. Heat is the most dependable and easiest controlled source of power, and it has the great advantage of being available at any place any time where there is fuel. To use heat to produce power, fuel is either burned under a boiler and the steam generated in the latter is then made to drive the piston of an engine, or it is burned directly in the cylinder of an engine and so drives the piston.

In either case the reciprocating motion of the piston thus obtained is converted into rotary motion by means of the crankshaft; the power thus developed is easily converted into other powers as, for instance, hydraulic pressure, compressed air, and electricity. From this you will see that by combining two or more substances by burning them the chemical energy can be released to furnish power.

The Meaning of Temperature.—When you pick up an object you say it is *warm* or *cool*, or *hot* or *cold*, but why do you say it and what do you mean by it? Just this. The chemical action going on in your body heats it to about 98 degrees Fahrenheit and if the object that you say is *warm* or *hot* is heated more than your body, it gives heat to you until the temperatures are the same. If the object feels *cool* or *cold* then the heat of your body is imparted to it until the heat of both is equalized. This extent of the heat of objects and things in general is called its temperature and it is measured in *degrees.*

To Measure Temperature.—The degree of heat of a body, that is the temperature of it, is measured by that familiar little instrument called a *thermometer*. This device consists of a glass tube having a very small bore and with a bulb on its lower end. The bulb is then filled with mercury and the upper end of the tube is sealed off. The tube is mounted on a *scale* having the *degrees* marked on it. Now mercury is a metal that remains a liquid at ordinary temperatures and like all other metals, except certain alloys, it expands when it is heated and contracts when it is cooled, hence it rises and falls in the tube as the temperature of the air, or whatever it is in contact with, changes.

The way the scale of a thermometer is marked off into degrees so that it will show the difference of temperature accurately, and hence measure it, is by placing the thermometer in melting ice and then marking off the point where the mercury has fallen in the tube, and this is the freezing point. This done, it is placed in boiling water and the point marked off where the mercury has risen in the tube, and this is the boiling point. The scale between these two points is divided into an equal number of spaces and a few like spaces are marked off above and below the freezing and boiling points.

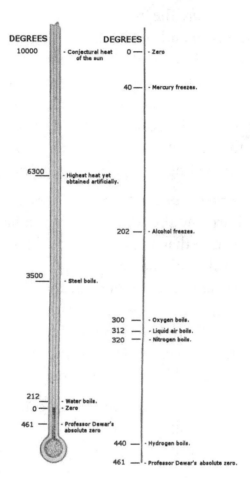

THE EXTREMES OF TEMPERATURE

This thermometer shows a variation from 10,000 degrees of heat to absolute zero, 461 degrees below our Fahrenheit zero. This is over 400 degrees below the point where mercury freezes.

Two kinds of thermometer scales are in general use in the United States, namely the *Centigrade scale* and the *Fahrenheit scale*. The freezing point on a Centigrade scale is marked *0* and the boiling point *100* and the scale in between is divided into 100 equal spaces. This thermometer is used for scientific work. The freezing point of a Fahrenheit scale is marked *32*, and the boiling point *212*, hence the scale is divided into 180 equal parts. This thermometer is in use for domestic purposes generally, among English-speaking peoples.

The Chemistry of Fuel.—Substances of any kind which will burn and thus develop heat can be used for fuels. A substance that makes a good fuel is one whose constituents will combine easily with the oxygen of the air, gives off a large amount of heat, and is so plentiful that it is cheap. The best fuels are those which are formed chiefly of carbon and hydrogen, for when these combine with the oxygen of the air they develop large amounts of heat and leave little or no ash behind.

When *hydro-carbons*, as fuels which contain carbon and hydrogen are called, burn they give off water vapor and carbon dioxide. If the burning process is not perfect then some of the carbon will pass off into the air and it is this visible product that we call *smoke*. Other foreign substances in fuels such as particles of rock and other minerals are left behind in the form of ashes.

And now let us find out what happens when fuel burns. In the first place, the hydrogen in it is set free and when this burns it makes a flame, or blaze. Then the carbon is heated to incandescence and combines with the oxygen of the air to make carbon dioxide which also passes off into the air. When a fire burns there is nothing wasted so far as nature is concerned, for the weight of the gases given off and the ashes that remain exactly equal that of the fuel used, plus the oxygen absorbed from the air.

Kinds and Qualities of Fuels.—Solid Fuels.—There are many kinds of fuels but all of them may be classified under three general heads, namely those that are solid, those that are liquid, and those that are gaseous. Wood, peat and coal are the chief solid fuels, petroleum and alcohol are the most widely used liquid fuels, while natural and manufactured gases are the chief gaseous fuels.

Wood was the first substance used for fuel and it furnished the only source of heat for mankind throughout the ages until some two centuries ago. Then came the discovery of coal and later petroleum. Wood for fuel is obtained by cutting down trees, but before it is used it must be *seasoned*, that is it must be split and piled up so that the water in it will dry out. Wood consists largely of *cellulose* (see Chapter X on *Paper Making*), a substance made up of carbon, hydrogen and oxygen. Hard wood is preferable to soft wood for fuel, for the harder it is, the longer it lasts.

Wood charcoal is simply charred wood. There are two ways of making it. In the older way cordwood is built up in a conical pile which is then covered with a layer of dirt. Some small holes are made through the layer at the bottom and a large hole is made through the top so that enough oxygen will be supplied to the wood to drive out the water, gases, alcohol, and acetic acid in it, but not enough to make the carbon combine, and, hence, nearly pure carbon in the form of charcoal remains. A more recent method of making charcoal is to heat the wood in a closed iron retort without any air whatever, and in this way the alcohol and other products of the wood can be saved.

COKE OVENS NEAR ALTOONA, PA
These ovens are filled from overhead with soft coal. The doors are sealed during firing.

FIRE, HEAT, AND FUEL

Peat is a kind of fuel that we who live in the United States know little about, but in Ireland and some other European countries it is used extensively. Peat is partly decayed vegetable matter so that it is neither wood nor coal. It is composed chiefly of moss which, when it dies, furnishes a bed for a new growth. As these various growths die they form a thick layer and this then breaks up under the action of the water that covers it into loose particles. Before it can be used for fuel it is cut out of the peat bog and laid in the sun to dry out. It then has somewhat the appearance of coal but different from the latter, nearly one-third of it is oxygen. It also contains a great deal of mineral matter which of course remains behind as ashes.

When the world was young, that is to say in the *carboniferous period*,[4] extensive areas were covered with swamps, the air was heavy and the temperature was tropical. This climatic condition caused ferns to grow in size as large as our present-day trees and as they died they were covered with water and underwent a process of partial deoxidation, or removal of oxygen. Then the great storms covered them over with soil and rock, and the pressure forced the gases out of them and left more or less pure carbon, or coal.

There are two kinds of coal in use: *bituminous*, or soft coal, and *anthracite*, or hard coal. The difference between them is that bituminous coal contains a great

---

[4]This is believed to have been about eighteen million years ago, when there were great swamps and fern forests and the first reptiles appeared.

deal of gas and many other substances including tar, and about whose marvels we shall tell you later.

Anthracite coal is formed chiefly of carbon, because the pressure of the soil on it was sufficiently great to force out the gases and other matter, leaving practically pure carbon behind, hence it burns with little flame. By enclosing bituminous coal in a closed retort and heating it, coke results, just as charcoal results when wood is burned in a retort. Also the various by-products can be recovered from it including the valuable coal tar which was once thought to be worthless and was thrown away.

Liquid Fuels.—Of the liquid fuels crude *petroleum* and *alcohol* are the most widely used. Crude petroleum, so called from the Latin words *petra* which means *rock* and *oleum* which means *oil*, is a thick, heavy oil from which fuel and other oils and products are obtained. It was first discovered in Pennsylvania but it has since been found in nearly every country on the globe. It is held in pockets in what is called oil bearing sandstones, hence the name petroleum, or *rock-oil*, and in conglomerates known as oil sands.

These oil pockets, or pools, are usually at considerable depths from the surface of the earth and to reach them wells are drilled through the intervening strata of earth. To separate the various oils from the crude petroleum it must be distilled, or refined, as it is called, and instead of doing this at the oil fields it is done at other places. Thus the petroleum obtained in the oil regions of Oklahoma is pumped through a pipe line to refineries in New Jersey.

At these refineries there are great stills and into these the crude petroleum is put, and heated. As each of the various oils in the petroleum has a different boiling point they pass off in vapors at different temperatures. This is what is called *fractional distillation*. In this way, then, the *gasoline*, *benzine* and *kerosene*, which are light oils are produced. Then there are the heavier oils used for lubricating, vaseline, and paraffin, while at the bottom of the still after the run is made a very hard cake remains.

Alcohol for fuel is made by fermenting grains, or other starchy materials, and molasses and sawdust. It is largely formed of hydrogen, hence burns with a colorless flame which is free from soot and has a high heat value. It makes an exceedingly convenient fuel where a small, hot flame is needed and it is sufficiently explosive to use in internal combustion engines.

Gaseous fuels may be either *natural* or *manufactured*. *Natural gas*, like petroleum with which it is usually associated, is found in airtight pockets in various localities. It is always under pressure and by drilling wells it issues forth in a stream. In the districts where it is found it is used exclusively as a fuel, for it is at once cheap and has a high fuel value. Illuminating gas is made either by heating soft coal in closed retorts when it is called *coal gas*, or by forcing a stream of air over the coal after it has been heated to incandescence, when it is called *water gas*.

CHAPTER IV

SOME USEFUL ACIDS

IF you ask the average person what an acid is he will more than likely tell you that it is a liquid with a sour taste, which will eat away metals and burn the skin. Now while all acids are sour, they are not all liquids until they are dissolved in water nor will all of them corrode metals. Chemically acids are compounds which contain *hydrogen* and a part, or all of which, can be exchanged for a metal. Nearly all acids contain *oxygen* as well as hydrogen and these two gases are combined with a third element. For instance, when hydrogen and oxygen and sulphur are combined we have the familiar *sulphuric acid*.

How Acids Behave.—If you will turn back to the second chapter you will notice that it says that water, which is *hydrogen* and *oxygen* combined, stands at the head of the class of solvents; that is to say, water will dissolve more substances than any other known liquid. It may surprise you a little to learn that water will even dissolve some of the lighter metals. But when it comes to the heavier metals such as iron and copper, silver and gold it takes a strong acid to dissolve them.

SOME USEFUL ACIDS

Why Acids Were So Named.—Whenever you find two or more things that have the same surname you can take it for granted that they are alike in some particular respect. For instance a fox-terrier and a bulldog do not look any more alike than a cat and a rabbit, but the former have anatomical points in common, so they are both called by the generic name of *dog*. This scheme also holds good for acids, and all acids, whether they are gaseous, liquids or solids, resemble all other acids in some specific way.

After oxygen was discovered it was believed by the early chemists that all acids must contain this gas. As the word *oxygen* means *acid former* all substances that contained oxygen if they would turn *blue* litmus paper *red* (this is a simple test for an acid) were called *acids*. Later on chemists found that all acids did not contain oxygen, as, for instance, *hydrochloric acid*, which is formed of *hydrogen* and *chlorine*. This is a gas and to use it, it is dissolved in water.

On the other hand, *sulphuric acid* is formed of hydrogen, sulphur and oxygen, while *nitric acid* is formed of hydrogen, oxygen, and nitrogen. From this you will see that while these three acids contain hydrogen only two of them contain oxygen. So after all, hydrogen is the real acid former; and hence, it follows that if a substance has no hydrogen it is not an acid. However, before an acid becomes active enough to dissolve metals and some other substances it must itself be dissolved in water.

Three Useful Acids.—There are numerous acids

but there are three common ones which are used in enormous quantities and for a large variety of purposes. These are *sulphuric acid, hydrochloric acid* and *nitric acid*. Between four and five million tons of sulphuric acid are made every year, while over one hundred thousand tons of nitric acid are made annually, and the amount of hydrochloric acid does not fall far short of the nitric acid output. So these are useful acids to know about.

About Sulphuric Acid.—To know about sulphuric acid we must start at the beginning and that is with *sulphur*. This element is found in nature mixed with earth and rock, and to get it in a pure condition the matter with which it is mixed is heated, when the sulphur melts and flows off as a liquid. On cooling, the crude sulphur is refined by distilling it when it again liquefies and is run into molds. This gives it the form of a roll and this is the *roll sulphur* we buy in the drug store.

Now sulphur will combine with the various metals in very much the same way that oxygen does. When it combines with copper a new and very different substance results which is called *copper sulphide*. When copper sulphide is burned the sulphur of it combines with oxygen and makes a gas known as *sulphur dioxide* and this is formed of *equal* parts of sulphur and oxygen; the solid part that remains behind is *copper oxide*.

To make the sulphur dioxide take on more oxygen it is passed through a tube containing *powdered platinum* and this is heated to about 800° Fahrenheit. This *catalytic agent* makes the sulphur dioxide take on an additional half part of oxygen when the compound becomes *sulphur trioxide* which is a liquid and this is the basis of sulphuric acid. To make sulphuric acid, all that is needed is to pour the sulphur trioxide into some water. As sulphur trioxide and water have a great affinity for each other, the instant they come in contact the resulting solution, which is sulphuric acid, fumes and sputters as though a piece of red-hot iron had been dropped into it.

Just a word now about the catalytic agent. When the sulphur dioxide is passed over the heated platinum the latter does not combine in any way with it but simply helps the oxygen which is supplied by admitting air to the tube to unite with the sulphur dioxide. To such substances as help along the chemical action of other substances but which do not themselves enter into combination with them, the word *catalizer*, or term *catalytic agent*, has been given.

Some Properties of Sulphuric Acid.—Pure sulphuric acid is an oil-like liquid and it is often called *oil of vitriol* because it was made by the early chemists of *green vitriol* as they termed *sulphate of iron*. It is nearly twice as heavy as water with which it combines vigorously in all proportions. In mixing them always pour the acid into the water, a little at a time, and stir constantly. When the water is poured into the acid heat in large quantities is generated and if they are being mixed in a bottle an explosion may take place. Because it has a high boiling point it is largely used in making various other kinds of acids.

Sulphuric acid acts chemically on most metals, particularly zinc. It chars paper, wood and other substances, by *dehydrating* them, that is drying them out by extracting the hydrogen and oxygen in them which would combine to form water. It is this dehydrating action of sulphuric acid that makes it so very hard to heal burns caused by it. On the other hand, owing to its dehydrating action it is used extensively in various manufacturing processes.

Uses of Sulphuric Acid.—In the beginning of this chapter we mentioned that over four million tons of sulphuric acid are made and used in the United States and it keeps between one hundred and fifty and two hundred plants busy turning out this amount. Of this tremendous output the largest amount goes into the manufacture of fertilizers, and the second largest amount is used in refining petroleum. Then comes a long line of important processes in which it is used in one way or another, such as making aluminum sulphate and other sulphates, and in converting various substances into high explosives. Indeed, nearly every chemical process, however important or insignificant, uses sulphuric acid or some chemical which was made with sulphuric acid.

About Hydrochloric Acid.—In the early days, *hydrochloric acid* was made from the brine of the sea and it was called *muriatic acid*, a name that artisans still prefer to call it. You can make a little hydrochloric acid by putting a tablespoonful of common table salt, which is *sodium chloride*, into a test tube and filling the latter half-full of water. Next pour a little concentrated sulphuric acid into the test tube a drop at a time when it will fall to the bottom and come in contact with the salt. Very soon bubbles of gas will be formed. Let this action go on until it stops. Now fill the test tube up with water, and you will then have a small quantity of hydrochloric acid.

This is the chemical action in the above experiment: When you poured the sulphuric acid on the table salt, or *sodium chloride*, it reacted on it and formed *sodium sulphate* and at the same time *hydrogen chloride* gas was given off. Five hundred volumes of this gas will dissolve in one volume of water, so instead of escaping it is dissolved by the water and the resulting solution is hydrochloric acid.

Some Properties of Hydrochloric Acid.—When you buy chemically pure hydrochloric acid you get a solution that contains about forty per cent of hydrogen chloride gas dissolved in about sixty per cent of water. Hydrochloric acid that is sold for ordinary purposes contains various kinds of impurities and this gives it a dingy color; this kind is known as *commercial* hydrochloric acid, or muriatic acid.

While hydrochloric acid by itself will not dissolve gold or platinum and while it reacts on silver, copper, lead and mercury only feebly, it attacks zinc violently. With nitric acid it makes the *aqua-regia* of old, or *royal water*, so called because it dissolves gold, the "king of metals." Curiously enough, while hydrochloric acid is a poison, *gastric juice*, which is the chief digestive fluid of the stomach, is formed of a solution of very dilute hydrochloric acid, lactic acid and pepsin.

Uses of Hydrochloric Acid.—This acid is used in enormous amounts for making *chlorine* and, of the latter gas, bleaching compounds are made. It is also largely used for pickling iron preparatory to tinning it, and for making glue and gelatine.

About Nitric Acid.—It is easy to make a little nitric acid, for all you have to do is to put one ounce of *Chili saltpeter*, which is *sodium nitrate*, in a two-ounce glass retort with a stopper in it and then pour three-fourths of an ounce of sulphuric acid on it. Now fix the retort over a stand so that you can heat it over an alcohol lamp or a Bunsen burner and slip a test tube over the open stem of the retort.

Next heat the retort, when a chemical reaction takes place and the nitric acid will pass off as a vapor; to condense it into a liquid let some cold water run on the stem of the retort and nitric acid will drip into the test tube. In making nitric acid what takes place is that when the sodium nitrate and the sulphuric acid are heated together they react and form two new substances, which are *sodium sulphate* and *nitric acid*, the first of which remains behind as a solid in the retort and the last passes off as a vapor which is then liquified by cooling it with water.

In making nitric acid on a large scale the same process is used as in the previous experiment. The mixture of sodium nitrate, or niter as it is called, and sulphuric acid is heated in an iron retort and an even temperature is maintained in order to prevent the nitric acid as it is formed from breaking up. Before all of the sulphuric acid in the retort has been used the heat is cut off and this leaves some of the sodium nitrate behind. This with the sodium sulphate forms what is called *niter cake* and this by-product makes a good fertilizer. The nitric acid vapor is passed through a number of condensers in which it is cooled until it becomes a liquid.

Some Properties of Nitric Acid.—When pure, nitric acid is colorless but usually it has a yellow tint due to the presence of a lower oxide of nitrogen and other impurities in it. To clear it of these and hence make it colorless, a blast of air is forced through it which removes whatever gases there may be in it. Nitric acid is about one and one-half times as heavy as water, and when it makes contact with the air it fumes. On heating nitric acid it breaks up into oxygen and *nitrogen peroxide* which is a reddish gas. Not only heat but sunlight decomposes it to the extent of setting enough of the latter gas free to discolor it.

Nitric acid is a very poisonous and corrosive liquid and in the early days of chemistry it was called *aqua fortis*, which means strong water. It gives up its oxygen easily and consequently it is a powerful oxydizing agent, especially when it reacts on vegetable and animal matter. Like hydrochloric acid it reacts on most metals, but alone it will not dissolve gold or platinum; to do this it must be mixed with hydrochloric acid, as has been already explained. It has long been used as a test for gold, imitation jewelry and "gold bricks." Finally it produces very severe burns when it makes contact with living animal tissues and hence you must handle it with extreme care.

Uses of Nitric Acid.—You can gain some idea of the importance of nitric acid when you know that over one hundred tons of it are made and used yearly. Fifty years ago the use of nitric acid was almost limited to dyeing goods yellow, in surgery for cauterizing the flesh, and for etching the lines in copper-plate engraving, designs on razor blades, swords, etc. Now there are a dozen or more separate and distinct uses for it directly and indirectly.

From it are made *potassium nitrate, nitrocellulose, fertilizer, nitroglycerine* and *trinitrotoluol*, or *TNT*, as it is called. Potassium nitrate is used for preserving meat, making gunpowder and as a medicine. Nitrocellulose is made into guncotton, celluloid and collodion. As a fertilizer it makes food. Nitroglycerine is an explosive, aids in making dynamite and as a medicine; while the guncotton so produced is used in mines, torpedoes, etc., and it is the chief factor in making smokeless powder. Celluloid is used for photographic films, toilet articles, knitting needles, and transparent glass; and collodion is used in surgery and as a coating for photographic films. Finally trinitrotoluol is the explosive substance used in shells, bombs and torpedoes.

Extracting Nitric Acid from the Air.—Away back in 1781 Cavendish, one of the early chemists, discovered that whenever he made hydrogen and oxygen combine, the water that resulted always contained a trace of nitric acid. It is now one hundred and forty years since this

SOME USEFUL ACIDS

classic experiment was made, but the outcome of it has been that latter-day chemists are able to *fix* the nitrogen in the air, that is to make the nitrogen combine with the oxygen so that nitric acid would result. To-day there are several large plants where the *fixation of atmospheric nitrogen* is carried on on a large scale. These plants are, however, all near large water powers, as cheap power must be had in order to produce the nitric acid from the air at as low a price as that which can be made from Chili saltpeter.

Although four-fifths of the air is nitrogen, the hardest part has always been to extract, or *fix* it, in large quantities and at a low cost. As you learned in the first chapter the nitrogen and oxygen of the air will combine only when these gases are heated to something like 8,000 degrees Centigrade; when raised to this high temperature they then combine and nitric acid results.

The way this is done is to blow the air through a pipe or chimney in which there is an electric arc, the hottest flame that has yet been produced on earth, when the heat changes a part of it into *nitric oxide*. When this is cooled more oxygen combines with it and this in turn forms *nitrogen tetroxide;* the latter then passes through a tower in which water trickles down, and on coming in contact with the water it is absorbed and reaches the bottom as nitric acid.

Some Other Acids.—There are a large number of other acids but the five below mentioned are, after sulphuric, hydrochloric and nitric acids, the most important.

Acetic Acid.—After apple juice stands for some time it begins to ferment when *alcohol* is produced and this makes *cider* of it. The longer it stands the more it ferments, hence the more alcohol it has in it and the "harder" it gets. If allowed to stand long enough it gets sour and becomes vinegar. It gets sour because the alcohol is converted into *acetic acid*. This change is caused by numerous *Bacteria aceti*, a kind of bacteria, and it is these minute forms of life that make up the *mother-of-vinegar* which is found in the bottom of vinegar jars. Acetic acid for commercial purposes is obtained by heating wood in a closed retort, as explained in Chapter III, that is by the *destructive distillation* of wood.

Tartaric Acid.—Grapes contain an acid called *potassium tartrate* and this is commonly known as *tartaric acid*, or *cream of tartar*. While yeast is most generally used for making bread rise, *baking powder* comes next. The purpose of both yeast and baking powder is to liberate *carbon dioxide* and it is this gas when set free that really causes the dough to rise. Baking powder is usually made of *tartaric acid* and *sodium bicarbonate;* the former, together with the moisture in the dough, acts on the latter when it sets free its carbon dioxide.

Carbolic Acid.—The chemical name of carbolic acid is *phenol* and it is a coal-tar product, that is it is extracted from coal-tar. To separate it from the coal-tar the latter is treated with *caustic soda*, that is sodium hydroxide, which dissolves it out. Carbolic acid is best known as a *disinfectant* and it is a good one because it violently attacks matter that is decomposing. Practically all the carbolic acid that we used before the Great War was imported from abroad and so as soon as war was declared in 1914 our supply was cut off. It was then that Edison came to the fore and put up plants for making *synthetic phenol*, the process of which you will find described in a later chapter.

Hydrofluoric Acid.—This is an exceedingly curious acid and it is made of a curious element. The only known element that will not unite with oxygen is *fluorine*, but it will unite with hydrogen and when it does so *hydrofluoric acid* results. The peculiarity of hydrofluoric acid is that it has a very corrosive action on glass, that is it dissolves out the *silica*, which is the sand, in the glass and hence, it is used for etching designs on bottles and other glassware. Since it will eat glass it must be kept in paraffin, rubber or lead bottles. When it is mixed with water it is poisonous, and as even a drop of it may cause an ulcer if it gets on your hand you must handle it with extreme care.

Picric Acid.—In the early part of the war there was a great scarcity of *picric acid*, or *trinitrophenol*, to give it its chemical name. Picric acid is formed by the action of nitric acid on carbolic acid, that is phenol. In times of peace it is largely used as a dye for silk and wool as it colors these materials a rich yellow. In times of war picric acid is used as the explosive product for charging *lyddite* and *melonite* shells.

CHAPTER V

OLD METALS AND NEW ALLOYS

Just as the use of fire set early man above the ape-like man in intelligence, so the use of metals marked the development of his progress and, hence, of his civilization. At first he was only able to use those metals that are found free in nature, such as copper, gold and silver, and as the former metal was the most plentiful as well as the best adapted for making tools and implements it was the first to come into general use. When early man was able to discard his stone tools for copper ones the first great stride toward civilization was made.

But copper is too soft a metal to be made into really successful tools, and it was not until man had found a way to extract iron from the oxide it is combined with that the present great era—the iron and steel age—dawned and that was not more than two hundred years ago. The copper age and the iron and steel age, then, roughly mark the great periods through which mankind has progressed and is progressing in his onward march of civilization.

About Copper and Its Ores.—This metal is found *free*, or *native*, that is in practically a pure state in some parts of the world, especially in the Lake Superior region. Some of the mines in this district are very ancient and stone implements have been unearthed in them that belonged to a race who lived there before the Indians. But copper is found chiefly in ores, that is in the form of *copper sulphide* mixed with rock, and small amounts of lead, silver and gold are often included in it. In order to separate the copper from the ore the latter must be crushed and smelted. When a piece of pure copper is polished it has a rich reddish-brown color; but while copper does not rust like iron, it soon takes on a coating of oxide, sulphide or carbonate depending on which one of these elements has reacted with it.

The way copper sulphide is formed is thus shown: take a test tube, put some sulphur in it and heat it over an alcohol lamp or a Bunsen burner until it boils. Now dip a strip of copper into the test tube when it will take on a dull black color. On removing the strip you will find that it is no longer copper and it is certainly not sulphur. What has happened is that the copper and the sulphur have combined chemically and in so doing a new substance has been formed, which is *copper sulphide*. If now you will heat the copper sulphide to a high enough temperature to melt the copper, the sulphur will be driven off and pure copper will remain behind. This then is the way that nature makes copper sulphide and the way man recovers the copper from it.

Extracting the Copper from Its Ores.—As the *copper sulphide*, or other copper ore, is mixed up with rock, the first thing to do is to *concentrate* it, which in the early days of copper mining was done by hand, and it is sometimes done in this primitive fashion even now at small mines, but generally it is done in *stamp mills*. After the ore has been concentrated there are two ways in which the copper can be extracted from it: (1) by *smelting*, and (2) by *leaching*.

Smelting Copper Ores.—The first thing that is done where the ore is to be smelted is to pile it up in a heap, or put it in a kiln, and heat it, or *roast* it as it is called. This drives off a large part of the sulphur and other foreign matter in the form of gases. Next the ore thus treated is put into a blast furnace, or a *reverberatory furnace*,[5] where it is heated to a high enough temperature to fuse the mass with coke and this yields a *matte*, that is the crude copper and a slag formed of all the impurities. These are easily separated for since the slag is the lightest it floats on the molten copper which is then drawn off into bars. This method of smelting is known as the *reduction process*.

Wet Method of Extraction.—This method, which is called *leaching*, is used only where there is a very small per cent of copper in the ore. In this case the ore is piled up high and under the action of air and water the copper oxidizes, when it is washed out by forcing water through the pile. The copper is then *precipitated*, that is thrown down, when it is collected, and melted and refined in a furnace and cast into ingots.

[5]This kind of a furnace has a vaulted ceiling that throws back the heat and flame on the surface of the molten metal.

Refining of Crude Copper.—After the copper is extracted by one or the other of the processes described above it still contains many impurities and, hence, it is called *crude copper*. To remove as much of the foreign matter that still remains in it as possible, the copper is placed in a *reverberatory* furnace where it is melted and a blast of air is forced across the surface to oxidize it. Then it is *poled*, that is it is stirred with greenwood poles while it is melted and this process brings a large amount of the impurities to the surface. To obtain really pure copper, however, it must be refined by the *electrolytic process*, and much of it is refined in this way at the present time. This process is described in Chapter XIII, under *Electro-chemical Processes*.

Some Uses of Copper.—Copper is a very ductile and malleable metal and next to silver it is the best conductor of heat and electricity. Now while heating iron and dipping it into cold water hardens it, it does just the reverse with copper, that is it softens it. When copper burns it gives forth a peculiar green flame that is always easy to recognize. In order to dissolve it you must use nitric acid.

Copper is used for so large a number of purposes it would take a chapter to tell all of them; in fact it has a larger number of uses than any other metal excepting iron. Large quantities of it are used in the electrical industries, as for instance wire for winding dynamos and motors, telephone wires and cables, electric light and trolley lines. Hundreds of uses are found for sheet copper from making coffee pots to making distillery stills. It is used for roofing and for many other purposes where air and water or both would attack other metals. Among its interesting uses are for electroplating and electrotyping and these will be described in the chapter on *Electro-chemistry*. Finally it enters into the composition of a large number of alloys, of which the following are a few:

Copper Alloys.—When two or more metals are melted and mixed together, they form a new metal whose properties are often very different from either of the metals used. *Brass*, which has nearly as wide a range of usefulness as copper, is formed of copper and zinc, the proportions varying according to the use to which it is to be put. The amount of copper ranges from sixty to ninety per cent. *Bronze* is made up of from seventy to ninety per cent of copper, one to twenty-five per cent of zinc and one to ten per cent of tin. *Bell* metal is a kind of bronze.

Phosphor-bronze is very hard and springy and is not affected by water; it is formed of copper with a small trace of phosphorus in it. *German silver* contains from fifty-two to sixty per cent of copper, eighteen to twenty per cent of nickel and twenty per cent of zinc; as this alloy has a high electrical resistance, the wire is largely used in electrical apparatus. *Gun metal* has ninety per cent of copper and ten per cent of tin in it. *Silver coins* have ten per cent of copper and ninety per cent of silver in them. *Nickel coins* are made of seventy-five per cent of copper and twenty-five per cent of nickel, and *gold coins* contain eight and thirty-three-hundredths per cent of copper.

OLD METALS AND NEW ALLOYS

About Iron and Steel—If all other metals in the world were wiped out of existence and iron alone remained, we could manage to get along very well. Gold, silver and platinum are metals that make for luxury, though they have their practical uses too, but iron is the constructive metal of the world and as such its uses range all the way from the microscopic screws used in watches to the skeleton frames of skyscrapers.

Different from nearly all the other metals, iron is found in every country on the face of the earth so that each nation has a supply of its own. All they need to do is to mine the ore, melt the metal out from it, and work it up into things that make for the highest kind of civilization. Unlike copper, iron is seldom found native, that is in the metallic state, and this is the reason its use was so long delayed. It needed time and required genius to take the ore and extract the iron from it. But when it was once done the development of the metal went forward at a rapid pace and invention paralleled its progress.

Smelting Iron Ores.—The process used to make the ore give up the iron locked in it is a simple one. A blast furnace is built up of stone or brick or iron and lined with fire clay. A runway is built over the top of the furnace so that the fuel and ore and limestone can be dumped into it in alternate layers. At the bottom of the furnace is a pipe, called a *tuyère*, through which a blast of air is forced, hence the name *blast furnace*. The air blast supplies the extra oxygen necessary to raise the temperature of the burning fuel to a point where it will melt the iron. At the bottom of the furnace below the air blast pipe is a *slag* hole through which the slag is run off, and below the slag hole is the *tap hole* through which the molten iron is run off.

In the action that takes place the limestone combines with the rock and other impurities and this forms a hard, glass-like slag. Since the molten iron is heavier than the slag it falls to the bottom of the furnace when, in the older plants, it runs off into a main channel, called the *sow*, that is cut into the sand floor. From the sow the iron runs into smaller channels that lead from and at right angles to it and these are called *pigs* and this is the way that *pig-iron* got its name. In more modern blast furnaces a mechanically operated ladle is filled with the molten iron and from this it is poured into successive iron molds which are mounted on an endless chain.

Kinds of Iron.—As iron is an element, of course, there is really only one kind when it is pure. But pure iron is almost unknown in the industries, and practically all of it that is used has some carbon in it. By *kinds of iron* are meant iron which contains different amounts, or percentages, of carbon, for varying amounts of carbon give to iron wholly different properties. There are three different kinds of iron and these are *cast iron*, *wrought iron*, and *steel*. Cast iron contains from two to five per cent of carbon; wrought iron about one-half of one per cent of carbon; and steel from one to two per cent of carbon.

Cast Iron.—When iron comes from the blast furnace it is hard and can neither be welded nor wrought. While nearly all metals contract upon cooling, iron expands and this property makes it especially useful for casting since it makes a sharp copy of the pattern. Cast iron can be *annealed*, that is made soft enough to be machined, by slowly cooling it, or very hard by pouring it into iron molds, or *chills* as they are called, and for this reason iron thus cast is known as *chilled iron*. It was long in use for making plowshares and burglar proof safes before steel became available.

Wrought or Malleable Iron.—When a current of highly heated air is passed over molten cast iron it burns out nearly all of the carbon in it, and in this way it is made into wrought iron. To get all of the slag out of the iron, it is hammered under a trip hammer while it is still red-hot and then rolled between rollers with grooves in them. When these operations are complete the iron is soft and can be worked and welded.

Steel.—Steel is made of cast iron by any one of a number of processes, but the purpose of all of them is to burn out a part of the carbon and to change that part which remains to *iron carbide*, hence there is no free carbon in the steel. Various kinds of steel have different amounts of iron carbide in them depending on the use to which they are to be put; thus we have *mild*, *half-hard*, and *tool* steels.

The Bessemer Converter Process.—Sir Henry Bessemer was the first to discover a way to make cheap steel. His process consists of a large crucible supported on pivots so that it can be tilted and the metal poured out. It is open at the top and an air-blast pipe connects with the inside at the bottom. A few tons of the best cast iron is melted and poured into the *converter*, as the crucible is called. A blast of air is now forced into, up and through the molten iron, when the oxygen of the former raises the temperature to a point where the excess carbon is burned out while the remaining carbon combines with the iron and forms iron carbide. The whole operation of converting iron into steel takes only about twenty minutes.

POURING LIQUID STEEL

Showing one operation of the Bessemer process for making indestructible steel, which is rolled into shape without hammering.

The Open Hearth Process.—In this process a shallow circular crucible is enclosed in a furnace heated by gas. The crucible is filled with pig-iron, steel scrap and iron ore, and the charge is brought to a molten state by heating it with a gas flame burning in a blast of air. It takes twenty-four hours to convert iron into steel by this process, but the steel so made is of a far better quality than that made by the Bessemer process.

The Crucible Process.—Where a fine and uniform steel is needed, as for tool-making or special alloys, the crucible process is used. In this process pure wrought iron and steel are placed in a large graphite crucible, together with a certain amount of charcoal. The crucible is then heated until the iron and steel in it are melted, when the additional carbon required is extracted from the charcoal. As only small quantities of steel can be made at a time by this process it is expensive.

The Electric Furnace Process.—This process bids fair to displace the crucible process just described, for not only can better steel be made by the latter than by the former, but it can be made in a shorter time and it is not so costly. The electric furnace has a shallow circular crucible like the open-hearth furnace, but instead of gas burning in an air blast it is heated by an electric arc formed between two carbon electrodes.

New Steel Alloys.—There are a number of new, interesting and highly useful alloys that are made by mixing certain metals with steel. For instance, by mixing from 2 to 4 per cent of nickel with steel, an alloy is made which is very hard and elastic and resists the action of sea-water. *Nickel steel,* as it is called, is used for undersea cables, propeller shafts for ships and armor-plate for battle-ships.

By adding 16 to 20 per cent of *tungsten,* ½ to ¾ per cent of carbon, 2½ to 5 per cent of chromium and ¼ to 1½ per cent of vanadium to steel, an alloy called *high-speed steel* results. This remarkable metal does not lose its temper even when it gets red-hot, hence it is used for making *high-speed* tools, and for this reason it is called *high-speed steel.*

Vanadium steel, or chrome vanadium steel, to give it its full name, has a high *tensile* strength, and while it is very springy it can be bent double without breaking. It is therefore largely used for making frames and springs for automobiles. It consists of 1 per cent of chromium and .15 per cent of vanadium mixed with the steel.

The hardest and most wear-resisting metal known is the alloy called *manganese steel.* It contains from 7 to 20 per cent of manganese and 1½ per cent of carbon. Owing to its great hardness it is used for switches and crossovers for railways, for the steel jaws of rock crushers, for burglar-proof safes, and the like.

About Aluminum.—Aluminum gets its name from *alum,* and it was first extracted by treating *aluminum chloride* with *metallic sodium.* It is contained in clay, slate, mica and feldspar rocks and next to oxygen and silicon there is more of it in the earth's crust than any other element. It has a bright silvery appearance; it does not tarnish when exposed to air, and weighs only about one-third as much as iron.

Notwithstanding there are such large stores of aluminum to draw from, for every bank of clay is full of it, it is hard to extract, for it is never found free. From the time the metal was obtained in 1845 by Deville, who made it by heating *aluminum chloride* with *metallic potassium*, it remained so costly (ninety dollars a pound) that a sample of it was looked upon as a curiosity.

This state of affairs continued until 1886, when Charles W. Hall, a young man of twenty-two who had just graduated from Oberlin College, found that by mixing *cryolite*, a mineral that melts at a low temperature and which is a poor conductor of electricity, with *beauxite*, an ore containing from 50 to 70 per cent of *aluminum oxide*, then melting them together, and passing a current through the solution, the aluminum oxide was decomposed and the metal aluminum was produced.

Uses of Aluminum.—The fact that this metal is so light, good to look upon, and that it is not affected by the air, makes it an admirable metal to use for cooking utensils, especially where these are for camping. Aluminum is a very good conductor of electricity and is largely used for cables in high-tension lines. It is also used for welding and making pure metals by the *thermit process*, besides having many other uses.

The Thermit Process.—Take a strip of aluminum and heat in an alcohol or a Bunsen flame, when you will find that before it gets red-hot, it will become coated with a thin layer of white powder which is *aluminum oxide*. Now take a bit of aluminum foil and hold it with your forceps in a jar of oxygen, and then touch a red-hot iron wire to it, when it will vanish in a bright flash leaving a white powder behind which is, again, aluminum oxide. When aluminum combines with oxygen it develops a temperature so high that it will melt any of the metals, and this is the principle on which the *thermit process* is based.

The thermit apparatus is very simple. It is a conical crucible with the small end down and whose bottom can be removed. Into this is placed a mixture of iron oxide and powdered aluminum with a fuse leading half-way into it from the top. When the fuse is ignited the aluminum combines with the oxygen of the iron oxide, and this generates enough heat to melt the iron which then falls to the bottom of the crucible, where it can be run off into a mold. In this way not only pure iron or steel can be had but broken castings can be repaired. When the oxides of other metals are placed in the crucible the metals are melted in the same way.

CHAPTER VI

GASES, GOOD AND BAD

GASES are very much like little boys, in that some of them are very, very good and some of them are horrid. In the first chapters we discussed nitrogen, oxygen and hydrogen. These are *good gases* because they serve useful purposes. Besides these there are many others, but you should know particularly about three of them:

The Gas Called Ammonia.—When you go to the grocers and buy ten cents' worth of *ammonia* you get a bottle filled with a transparent liquid, and if you uncork it you will find it has a very pungent odor. This bottled ammonia is, however, only water with a very little *ammonia gas*—for ammonia is a gas—dissolved in it. Since this is the case it should be and often is labeled *aqua ammonia*, which means ammonia water, since *aqua* is Latin for water. Ammonia that you get at the drug store is very much stronger, as it has a larger per cent of ammonia gas dissolved in the water and if you smell of this it will nearly stifle you. This kind is called *concentrated ammonia*.

In the long ago ammonia gas was called *hartshorn* and ammonia in water was known as *spirits of hartshorn*.

Now a hart is a kind of a deer, and as ammonia was first made from the horns of a hart, it came by this queer name honestly. The name *ammonia* was given to it because *sal ammoniac*, one of its compounds, was first made near the Temple of Jupiter Ammon.[6]

Ammonia gas is plentiful, as it is formed when vegetable matter decays and, hence, even the air we breathe often contains considerable quantities of it, but it is obtained on a commercial scale as a by-product when coal-gas is made, that is when bituminous coal (soft coal) is subjected to destructive distillation in a closed retort. Now, soft coal contains both *nitrogen* and *hydrogen*, and when the coal is heated in the retort these two gases combine and form *ammonia gas*. This is, of course, mixed with the illuminating gas but is separated from the latter by passing them through water, when the ammonia gas is dissolved out and the solution that is left is called *ammoniacal liquor*.

You can make enough ammonia gas to detect the odor of it by heating any kind of lean meat, and bits of horn and hoofs of an animal, or vegetable matter in a closed glass retort over an alcohol or a Bunsen flame. To make ammonia in a laboratory, put a couple of ounces of *unslaked lime*, or *quick-lime* as it is called, together with a like amount of *ammonium chloride* in your mortar and mix them well. Now place the mixture in a retort and heat it, when you will soon detect the

---

[6] A temple in Egypt dedicated to the sun-god, Jupiter Ammon, who is represented as having the body of a man and the head of a ram.

odor of ammonia gas which passes out through the delivery tube.

The Properties of Ammonia.—Ammonia is a colorless gas, is about half as heavy as air and six hundred volumes of it will dissolve in one volume of water at about 70 degrees Fahrenheit. Ammonia will not burn in air at ordinary temperatures, but it burns with a greenish yellow flame in oxygen. Should you inhale a very little ammonia tears will flow, and should you get into a room where it is escaping it may suffocate you. It will neutralize any of the acids and in so doing forms various useful salts.

For example, to make *sal ammoniac*, all you need to do is to slowly pour a little *aqua ammonia* into *hydrochloric acid*; test the solution as you are making it with *litmus paper*, and when it no longer turns red you will know that it has been neutralized. Now heat the solution in a porcelain dish until it has evaporated, when only a white powder is left, and this is sal ammoniac.

The Gas Called Chlorine.—*Chlorine* belongs to the *halogen* family, the other members of which are *iodine*, *bromine*, and *fluorine*. These four elements are quite alike in many respects, and they got their family name *halogen* from *hals*, which means *salt*, from which chlorine is largely obtained; in fact, sixty per cent of common salt, that is, sodium chloride, is made up of this gas. To make chlorine you heat manganese dioxide, sodium chloride and sulphuric acid together, and when these react on each other manganese sulphate, sodium sulphate and water are formed and chlorine is liberated, the latter in large quantities.

Some Properties of Chlorine.—If you should ever smell chlorine you may doubt that it is one of the "good" gases, and if you are so unfortunate as to inhale some of it you will say that it acts like anything but a good gas, for a little of it will make you cough, and more will suffocate you. It was always known as a good gas, however, until the war broke out, and then it became the first of the bad gases, as you will presently see.

Chlorine and water get along very well together, and two volumes of the former will mix with one volume of the latter; if, now, this solution is exposed to the sunlight it will change into hydrochloric acid and oxygen. But chlorine loves hydrogen as a miser loves his gold, and it will extract it from any vegetable matter that contains it, and when these two gases combine they form hydrochloric acid.

Bleaching With Chlorine.—The great value of chlorine lies in its power to take the color out of certain kinds of materials, particularly cotton and paper, and this it does with great rapidity. This is because nearly all coloring matter, except printers' ink, contains hydrogen, with which it instantly combines. As printers' ink does not contain hydrogen it is not affected by it.

Owing to this peculiar property of chlorine for combining with hydrogen and so attacking coloring matter, it is largely used for bleaching both muslins and paper. Where muslins are to be bleached at home, the housewife begins by removing the grease from it, which she does by boiling it in water with soap. Then she lays the goods on the clean grass, when the hydrogen that is in the coloring matter combines with the oxygen of the air and the dew and so in due time the goods are bleached perfectly white. The goods are not only bleached but they are made sweet and clean.

Home bleaching as described above is a slow process, and so where muslins are to be bleached on a commercial scale a different process is used, though the principle is the same. First the grease is removed from the muslin by boiling it in water in which alkalis have been dissolved. This done, it goes through a solution of chloride of lime and water, and then through a weak solution of sulphuric acid. It is at this stage that the acid and the chloride of lime react and this sets free the chlorine; this then combines with the hydrogen that is in the coloring matter of the goods and hydrochloric acid is formed. In many cases the chlorine extracts hydrogen from the water, thus freeing oxygen, which in turn destroys the color. Large quantities of chlorine are used in paper mills to bleach the rags from which linen paper is made and also to bleach the wood pulp from which newspaper is made.

Chlorine as a Disinfectant.—Not only is chlorine a great bleaching agent but it is also a powerful disinfectant, and for the same reason. That is to say, it disinfects in exactly the same way as it bleaches, namely, by combining with the hydrogen; in the latter case the hydrogen is in the refuse or other disease-bearing matter and so breaking it up. A simple method of producing chlorine for the sick room is to place some chloride of lime in a saucer and moisten it with water. The gas is soon set free and begins its work of purification.

Helium, the New Gas.—Away back in the year of 1869 Professor Lockyer, a noted British astronomer, while examining the sun with his *spectroscope*,[7] discovered a gas which was at that time unknown on the earth, and he believed it to be an element that existed in the sun only; he called this gas *helium* from the Greek word *helios*, which means *sun*. A quarter of a century later Sir William Ramsay made a succession of brilliant researches which resulted in the discovery of *argon*, *neon*, *krypton*, and *xenon*, as explained in Chapter I, and as a final climax he discovered a gas that was identical with the *helium* of the sun discovered by Lockyer. Since they were alike, Ramsay also called the gas *helium*.

The way he made the discovery was thus: He was boiling *clévite*, a rare mineral, in some dilute sulphuric acid to find out whether the gas that was given off and which was believed to be *nitrogen* contained any argon. When, however, he examined the gas with his spectroscope, he found that instead of the gas being nitrogen it was helium. Since then a large number of minerals have been tested for helium and quite a number have been found to contain small quantities of it, as well as some gases.

Natural gas from the wells in various parts of the

---

[7] An optical instrument for analyzing the spectra of the rays emitted by substances and bodies. It was invented by the German physicists, Kirchhoff and Bunsen.

United States contains considerable quantities of it, and according to recent figures by experts it is escaping from them into the air at the rate of a million and a quarter cubic feet a day, which is enough to fill four large airships every week. The Government will probably acquire the rights to them, and the question of sealing them for future use is now being considered, as this would give the United States a monopoly, practically, of the world's chief sources of supply. The way in which helium is obtained from natural gas is to liquefy the latter, when the former still remains a gas.

The Use for Inflating Balloons.—Helium is a colorless gas and, next to hydrogen, it is the lightest gas known, having a lifting power of 50 per cent of the latter. Like argon and the other gases that Sir William Ramsay discovered in the atmosphere, helium is *inert;* that is it will not unite chemically with other elements. This being true, it will not burn and it is easy to see that it is an ideal gas with which to inflate spherical and dirigible balloons. The greatest difficulty is to obtain enough of it and at a price that would make its use practicable, and this the United States Navy has now done.

The first balloon in the world to be filled with helium was the *C-7*, a navy dirigible. On December 5, 1921, she was inflated with this gas at the naval air station at Hampton Roads, Va., when she was sailed to Washington and back. It was the first time in the history of aeronautics that the lifting power of helium was actually tried out and she met every test she was subjected to. It marked a great advance in airships for the gas could not ignite or explode, and, moreover, when she returned to her hangar at Hampton Roads she showed that not a particle of gas had escaped through the fabric of which the bag was made, whereas with hydrogen there is always some small leakage due to diffusion.

This pioneer test of the use of helium for inflating balloons and airships marks the passing of the highly inflammable hydrogen, for a gas that is perfectly safe, and in the near future we can expect the prohibition of the use of hydrogen alone for this purpose, as a mixture one-fourth helium is not inflammable.

A RIVAL FOR HELIUM

Curranieum is the name of a new gas discovered by E. Curran of Los Angeles. Like helium, it is non-flammable.

GASES, GOOD AND BAD

Some Bad Gases.—Gases we may call *bad* are the *killers;* that is, they are made and used purposely to destroy human life. This idea of making *poison gases*, as they are called, originated in Germany, and from the time the Great War began until it ended the Germans made and used over twenty different kinds.

The first poison gas was chlorine, which they used early in 1915 at Ypres, and they chose chlorine as being the safest for themselves as well as the most deadly for the Allies.

The way they used it was to wait until the wind was blowing over their own front and in the direction of the opposing front. Then they released great volumes of chlorine at intervals along their front and the wind carried the deadly fumes over to the French. As chlorine is two and one-half times heavier than air it rolled along the ground and when it came to the trenches they were filled with it. The soldiers in them were attacked by coughing, but soon they were suffocated. So deadly were the effects of the gas that only twenty per cent of the men were still alive and available for service after the air had dissipated the fumes.

By the time they next attempted to use chlorine the Allies were ready and met and warded off the death-dealing fumes with *gas-masks* which were prepared with alkali-carbonate, and this counteracted the effect of the gas. Since chlorine could not be easily controlled when it was used in this way, and also because the Germans found the Allies were able to defeat its use with gas-masks, they changed over to another poison-gas called *phosgene*.

This new poison gas was formed of *chlorine* and *carbon monoxide*, and instead of liberating it and letting the wind blow it over the lines of the Allies, they loaded shells with it and then fired them from guns and mortars, and the effect would have been more deadly than where free chlorine was used but for the fact that the British had learned through secret channels that they were going to use it. Thus forewarned the Allies had gas-helmets made with *hexamethylene tetramine* in them, and this counteracted the effects of the gas.

After this the Germans followed with the poison gas *benzyl bromide*, or *tear gas* as it was commonly called. This gas had a terrible effect on the eyes of the victims, making them water until they could not see and finally blinding them. They next used *diphenyl chloroarsine*, or *sneezing gas*, and this made its victims sneeze so hard they were compelled to take off their masks and so expose themselves to the deadly fumes.

While the Germans were trying out these various poison gases the Allies were busy inventing new ones in self-defense. Here in the United States enormous quantities of a gas called *chloropicrin* was made. The purpose of it was not so much to kill as to make the victims vomit, when they would have to take off their gas-masks. On doing so, they got a dose of *tin chloride* which suffocated them. This substance, which is formed of tin and chlorine, was loaded into the shell along with the *chloropicrin*, which is a compound of picric acid and chlorine, so that both gases were set free at the same time. It is doubtful if the Germans could make a gas-mask that would withstand the onslaughts of both of these gases.

The most painful poison gas that the enemy used, though not the most deadly, was *dichlorodiethylsulphide*, otherwise known as *mustard gas*, and at different periods of the war as many as fifty thousand shells filled with it were thrown in a single night into the trenches of the Allies.

This gas was formed of chlorine, alcohol and sulphur, and when these substances are combined they form a gas that is very penetrating and one which lasts a long time. It smells not so much like oil of mustard as it does like garlic, but it hurts the eyes like a mixture of them, only a thousand times worse. It attacks the victim's eyes, nose, throat and lungs and makes them burn and blister, and all the while the pain it causes is intense. The best thing that can be said about *mustard* is that if the victim can be treated immediately after being gassed with it he stands a fair chance of recovery.

CHAPTER VII

FROM GUNPOWDER TO TNT

We are apt to think of gunpowder and other explosives as belonging only to the arts of war, but they have many uses in the pursuits of peace as well. It is usual to give the Chinese the credit of having discovered *gunpowder* and it is quite certain that they made firecrackers with it at least two thousand years ago; what is more, they still make them, to the great joy of the American boy who likes above all things to "shoot them off" in celebration of our nation's birthday.

Marco Polo, the boy traveller, who visited China about twelve hundred years ago, saw there the explosive effects of the mysterious black substance, which was later named *gunpowder*, and he learned how it was made. On returning to Arabia some of it was made and its power tried out by firing it from a tube in which a stone was loaded. This, then, was the crude beginning of the gigantic guns that wrought such havoc during the World War.

About five or six hundred years after the Arabs made their first experiments with gunpowder as a weapon of war, other travellers took the art of making gunpowder into Italy and from there it found its way into Germany. The first time that gunpowder and cannon were actually used in warfare was in 1346 at the battle of Crécy, but they did not displace the long bow and bow-gun, or *arabesque*, as the latter is called, for many years after, and gunpowder remained the only explosive known until the last century, when nitroglycerine was invented.

How Gunpowder is Made.—Gunpowder is a simple mechanical mixture of *Bengal saltpeter*, that is *potassium nitrate*, sulphur and charcoal. Each of these substances is powdered and then all of them are thoroughly mixed together. Enough water is now added to the mass to make a paste of it, when it is allowed to stand until the water has dried out of it and a hard, black cake remains. The cake is then broken up into fine or coarse grains according to what the powder is to be used for. Where it is to be used for sporting guns of small caliber the grains must be very fine, while for guns of large caliber the grains must be proportionately large. To understand how and why gunpowder explodes you should know something about each of the ingredients that is used in it.

Potassium nitrate, which is also called *nitrate of potash, saltpeter* or just *niter* for short, is, as its name indicates, formed of nitrogen and potash. Saltpeter is found in India and in various other tropical countries but only in small quantities. It was formerly made by *leaching*, that is by piling up the refuse of stables and other decaying vegetable matter together with some mortar. Then at the end of two or three years the piles are washed out, when for every cubic foot of the matter some five ounces of saltpeter will be produced. During the War of 1812 saltpeter was made in Mammoth Cave, Kentucky, and to this day a part of the plant together with the tracks of the wagon wheels may still be seen there.

In Chili, South America, there are great beds of *sodium nitrate*, called *Chili saltpeter*, and in Stassfurt, Germany, there are even greater beds of *potassium chloride*, so chemists set to work to make *potassium nitrate* out of them. This they did by mixing the potassium chloride with a hot solution of sodium nitrate, when the following reaction takes place:

sodium nitrate plus *potassium chloride* yields *potassium nitrate* plus *sodium chloride*.

Charcoal, as you know, is made by heating wood in a closed retort. It is nearly pure carbon and has so many little pores that in a cubic inch of it there is nearly one hundred feet of surface. Sulphur is one of the earliest known elements and it played a great part in the experiments of the alchemists of old who vainly tried to transmute the baser metals into gold. It is found free in various countries, especially in the volcanic regions of Sicily. We get our supply chiefly from Texas and Louisiana, though it is mined in other parts of the United States.

When Gunpowder is Fired.—The explosive force of gunpowder is caused by the gases which are set free by the burning substances and which expand enormously. The instant the powder is ignited the saltpeter liberates its oxygen and the carbon and sulphur burn in it at white heat. The enormous heat developed makes the gases expand until, if they were free, they would take up a thousand five hundred times as much space as that which the powder originally occupied and this produces the force needed to drive the bullet from the barrel of the gun. One-third of the burned gunpowder is in a solid state and this passes off as smoke, except for a small part which is left behind in the barrel of the gun.

It is a part of these solid products of combustion of the powder that cling to the inside of the barrel of the gun and *foul* it, and unless the utmost care is taken to keep it clean the particles of matter will keep on building up until a hard crust is formed the entire length of it. Now since the bore of the barrel and the outside diameter of the bullet are practically the same, when the latter is forced through the former by the expanding gases the crust not only slows down the speed but also tears off bits of lead and these foul the gun still more.

Besides excessive fouling, another very bad feature of *black-powder*, as common gunpowder is called, is that the large volumes of dense smoke given off when it is used in large guns for military operations, show the enemy exactly where they are located. The search for an explosive that would do away with both the fouling and the smoke led to the invention of *smokeless powder*.

How Smokeless Powders are Made.—Smokeless powder is entirely unlike black powder in every respect except that it explodes. For instance, where the ingredients of black powder are merely mixed together, those of smokeless powder are chemically combined, and where black powder explodes on being ignited, smokeless powder explodes by *concussion*, that is when it is subjected to shock. This is because the chemicals of which it is made are very unstable compounds and a shock is enough to decompose them. As a matter of fact, smokeless powder is of two different kinds, the first of which is called *nitrocellulose powder* and the second is called *nitroglycerine powder*.

Nitrocellulose powder is made of *pyroxlin*, or *guncotton*, to call it by its common name. Guncotton, in turn, is made by treating pure cotton with nitric and sulphuric acids and then washing the excess of them out of it thoroughly. The acids dissolve away everything except the pure *cellulose*, which is the chief substance that makes up all kinds of plants, with which the strong nitric acid combines. For blasting purposes guncotton is sometimes made of *wood pulp*, from which print paper is also manufactured, but for military powders a good grade of cotton must be used. In either case after the guncotton has been made it is mixed with either *acetone* or ether and alcohol, when it becomes a dough-like mass. The next step is to feed it into a machine which rolls it out into rods and these are cut up into various sized grains according to what the powder is to be used for. Finally the grains are dried out thoroughly to expel the acetone or ether and alcohol.

Nitroglycerine powder is made of one-half *guncotton* and one-half *nitroglycerine*, or *glyceryl nitrate*, as the chemists call it. Nitroglycerine results when glycerine is treated with nitric and sulphuric acids. Nitroglycerine powder is not as well adapted for use in sporting guns as nitrocellulose powder, for it develops more heat and sets free acids which attack and pit the steel of the gun-barrels.

Smokeless powders have not only the advantage of developing practically no smoke but since they produce very small amounts of solid matter these are forced out of the gun-barrel by the gases. Smokeless powders are, however, more dangerous to use than black powder for they *detonate*, that is explode instantly, whereas black powder simply burns away.

Dynamite and Cordite.—*Dynamite* is made by mixing nitroglycerine with sawdust, flour or some other inactive material and then forming the mass into sticks. The inactive material is used to keep the molecules of the explosive as far apart from each other as possible, since this prevents the nitroglycerine from *detonating*, that is exploding instantly, hence there is less danger of its going off prematurely.

Cordite is an explosive that made millions for its inventor, Alfred Nobel, of Sweden. It is, in fact, a kind of smokeless powder, since it is made of guncotton and nitroglycerine mixed with a little vaseline. These three ingredients are dissolved in *acetone*, a substance that is obtained as a by-product when wood is distilled in a closed retort. After the ingredients have been dissolved in the acetone the resultant mass is rolled into sheets which are cut up into various-sized pieces. The final process consists of drying out the acetone, and when this is done a horn-like material results that goes by the name of *cordite*.

Lyddite, Melinite, and Shimose.—Another kind of high explosive is made from *phenol*, whose common name is *carbolic acid*. When phenol is heated with nitric and sulphuric acids yellow crystals are formed, and this substance is *trinitrophenol*, or *picric acid*. This acid is a high explosive, and in the early part of the World War it was one of the hardest substances to obtain. Picric acid is the chief ingredient that is used by the British in making *lyddite*, by the French in making *melinite* and by the Japanese in making *shimose*, all of which are practically one and the same thing. When the world is not at war picric acid is used as a dye for silk and wool.

What TNT is Made Of.—In experiments made by the British Government, it was found that the action of lyddite shells could not always be depended on, and that *trinitrotoluene*, or *TNT* (the first, fourth and ninth letters of the big name), as it is popularly called, gave more accurate results though it is not as powerful an explosive as picric acid. *TNT* is made by heating *nitric acid* and *toluene* when a reddish substance results that is related to benzene, or benzole.

When *TNT* explodes it forms water and sets carbon, hydrogen and carbon monoxide free, hence a dense black smoke is formed. For many purposes the smoke is not a disadvantage as, for instance, where it is used for the charging of the *warhead* of a submerged torpedo or filling shells that are fired from guns and which explode on striking the target. This is made possible because *TNT* will not explode by concussion, and so there must be some kind of a device which will ignite it at the proper time.

About Detonators and What They Do.—There are certain substances which when struck a sharp blow will instantly explode, or *detonate*, as it is called. A detonating substance of this kind is *mercuric fulminate*, and it is made by heating mercury with nitric acid, and on adding alcohol to the solution thus obtained a dense, white powder is thrown down. This powder, which is *mercuric fulminate*, is a very unstable compound, and it is largely used for firing, by shock, such explosives as nitroglycerine and smokeless powders, and for igniting black gunpowder, *TNT* and like explosives.

The fulminate powder after it is dried is mixed with gum arabic or some other binder and then made into *percussion caps*. Where large charges of explosives are to be set off, the cap is set inside of it, and when the hammer of the detonating mechanism strikes the cap a pin is driven against the mercuric fulminate which explodes it and it in turn either fires or explodes the charge.

There are several other and newer detonating substances and a compound called *tetryl*, which is made of *tetranitromethyl aniline*, is sometimes used instead of mercuric fulminate. Another detonating compound that has been used to some extent is *triazide*, which is made from *hydrazoic acid;* this acid is one of the most dangerous explosives known, as it explodes without the slightest apparent reason. Finally, the most powerful explosive that has yet been made is *tetranitroaniline*, and this is also used in detonators.

Peace-time Explosives.—The uses of explosives for war purposes were brought home to every man, woman and child during the great conflict, but there is another less known and more important use for them, now that peace reigns once more between the nations. In time gone by when a wooded land was wanted for farming purposes the trees were chopped down and the stumps were left to rot away—a method which required years. Then came the stump pullers, and this was an exceedingly hard and trying ordeal for both men and horses.

Now when wooded land is to be cleared, the trees are felled and the stumps are blown out either with dynamite or some other safe explosive. For road-making and excavating for foundations explosives also play a prominent part, while on the farm they are largely used for making holes for planting trees, and it is now a common practice among farmers and fruit growers to use them for breaking up the soil so that the air can reach it and fertilizers can be mixed with it.

Kinds of Farm Explosives.—The difference between explosives used in war operations and those used in peace-time pursuits is that the latter are not so dangerous to handle or so powerful as war material. The two chief kinds of explosives used for domestic work are *blasting powder* and *dynamite*. Blasting powder is nothing more nor less than black gunpowder, but it is not made as carefully or of materials as good as the powder used for sporting and military guns. It is, however, made in small and large grains so that the speed with which it burns can be varied, and therefore its explosive power can be controlled.

A dozen different blasting powders are made, the composition of each being the same, but the size of the grains of which range from particles almost as fine as flour to those as large as a bean. Where you want to loosen up the soil or break a rock into small pieces, a fine-grained powder is used, while if you want to lift out a stump or break away a large rock, then you should use a coarser grained powder.

Dynamite is more powerful than blasting powder and as it was the first of the high explosives to be extensively used it was called *dynamite* from the Greek word *dynamis*, which means *power*. An Italian chemist, Sobrero, first discovered nitroglycerine; this he did in 1847, but it was so dangerous that it was not used to any extent until twenty years after, when Alfred Nobel, the Swedish chemist, made it safer to handle by mixing it with *kieselguhr*, a kind of sandy earth. So popular did it become as a blasting agent, that it made the inventor a multimillionaire. Later on, sawdust, flour, magnesia, sodium carbonate and other *dope*, as these inert materials are called, took the place of kieselguhr. By varying the proportions of nitroglycerine and the *dope* that is used, different strengths of dynamite are obtained.

In making dynamite, enough dope is mixed with the

nitroglycerine to make it about as plastic as putty, and it is then pressed into sticks about two inches in diameter and eight inches long. Each stick is then wrapped in paper and paraffined to make it waterproof, when it is ready to blast out a few tons of coal or stone or lift a stump out bodily by the roots.

Firing Blasting Powder and Dynamite.—In the early days of blasting, the miners would drill a hole in the ore-bearing rock, fill it with black powder and then run a thin line of powder, called a *squib*, to a point some distance away; then they would light it and run to cover while the running was good. While this scheme was not very dangerous, still it was not any too safe, and moreover only one charge could be fired at a time.

An improvement on the squib is the *safety fuse*, that is, black gunpowder is twisted up in a strip of tape in the same way that the fuse of a firecracker is made. One end of the fuse is run into the bore-hole filled with powder and the other end is ignited. As it burns at about the rate of two feet a minute, the men who are using it know just how long it will take after the free end is ignited for it to reach the charge. Two or more charges of blasting powder can be fired at practically the same time by using an *instantaneous fuse;* this is so made that it burns at the rate of one hundred to three hundred feet per second.

A further improvement is the use of a *blasting cap* on the end of the fuse, and this is placed in the powder-filled bore-hole. Now when the sparks of the fuse reach the cap it explodes violently, and this in turn ignites all of the powder at the same instant which gives it more power.

The up-to-date way to fire charges of either black powder or dynamite is to employ an electric current. By doing so, the charge can be fired at exactly the moment desired and any number of charges can be exploded at once. Where a current is used, an *electric squib* or a *blasting cap* is connected to the end of a pair of insulated conducting wires which lead to a *blasting machine*.

An electric squib and a blasting cap are alike, except that the first has a paper shell and the latter a copper shell. In one end of the shell is placed a small explosive charge and into this a pair of insulated wires are run. The ends of the wires are connected with a very fine wire, called a *bridge*, and when a current passes through it the fine wire is heated and so ignites the charge.

The blasting machine is a small electric generator that is driven by hand power. It is made like the magneto of a motor car engine. The revolving element, which is called an *armature*, has a *pinion*, that is a small toothed wheel on it; a *rack*, which is a straight rod with teeth cut in it, meshes with the pinion. Now when a current is needed to fire the blasting cap, all that the blaster needs to do is to push down, firmly and quickly, on the handle.

CHAPTER VIII

HOW PLANTS LIVE AND GROW

AFTER water, the substance with which we are most familiar is the *land*, as the more or less solid part of the earth's surface is called, and as we live on and from it, it is worth while to find out how it is made and what it is made from. First of all, when the world was born, various elements and compounds united in enormous quantities and formed the solid substances that we call *rock*, and it is this that makes up the crust of the earth's surface.

Then began the endless action of the air and water on the rock, and these were ably assisted by the fierce heat of the sun and the intense cold of the glacial epochs, with the result that their combined forces throughout the ages broke much of it up, sometimes into giant boulders and at others into grains of sand. Thus it was that various kinds of land were made, and the process is still going on and will continue to go on to the end of the world.

The Various Kinds of Land.—Now the rock that forms the crust of the earth is of various kinds because different parts of it are formed of different elements which have united and produced them; thus *granite* is a very hard rock and is composed of *feldspar, mica,* and *quartz.* Feldspar and mica in turn consist of *silicate of aluminum* and some of the alkaline metals like potassium, while quartz is *silicon dioxide. Sand* is formed by the union of silicon and oxygen, and *sandstone* is sand cemented together, while *marble* and *limestone* are formed chiefly of *calcium carbonate.*

As these various kinds of rock were subjected to air and water and heat and cold, they produced a variety of land, the first of which is formed by the *rock* itself, the second is formed of *sand*, and the third is formed of *clay*. Then a fourth type of land is formed by a mixture of clay and sand, while on top of much of the land, or mixed with it, is the decayed animal and vegetable matter that has been accumulating through the countless centuries. It is this latter material that covers the land, or is mixed with it, that we are interested in, for this is the *soil* which makes it possible for plant life to flourish.

What is In the Soil.—The decayed animal and vegetable matter is called *humus*, and it is this substance that makes the kind of rich soil which is known as *loam*. Not only does the *humus* contain the chief substances on which plants live, but it holds the water and supplies it to the plants as they need it.

A soil of whatever kind contains many elements, but those that are absolutely needed for plant food are *nitrogen, phosphorus, potassium, sulphur, calcium, magnesium* and *iron*, together with *carbon, oxygen,* and *hydrogen* from the air and water. If any one of these ten elements is missing a plant cannot grow. *Virgin* soil, that is a soil which has never been used for growing plant foods before, contains all the above mineral elements, hence, for several years it will yield large crops. But after a time some of the elements, usually the nitrogen, phosphorus or potash, or all of them, become exhausted and the plants, deprived of a part of their food, will grow very poorly or not at all. This is the reason why farmers rotate their crops and use fertilizers.

The Action of Air on the Soil.—In raising crops, then, it is necessary to put back into the soil at least as much of the nitrogen, and other elements, as the plants have taken out of it for food, and this is one of the purposes of plowing and harrowing it. In this way the particles of the soil are loosened, allowing the air to circulate through it. In doing so, the oxygen comes into contact with the vegetable matter of which the humus is composed, and it is converted into soluble nitrogen compounds and phosphoric acid compounds. At the same time the carbon dioxide which is produced by decaying matter is caught by the water in the soil, and helps to render soluble some of the mineral matter.

The Action of Water on the Soil.—Plants cannot use gases, salts and acids direct for food, but these elements and compounds must be dissolved in water first. They are then in such condition that the plants can easily draw them through their roots, up and through their stalks and into their leaves. To do this, the roots, stalks and leaves of every plant are made up of little tubes called *capillaries*, and it is by and through these that the liquid foods are carried upward by *capillary attraction*, which is the same curious force that causes the oil in a lamp to *"soak up"* from the lower end of a wick dipping into it to the upper end, where it is lit. Since plants, like animals, are made up of three-fourths water, the soil supplies this amount to them while they are growing, as well as foods which are dissolved in it.

How the Soil is Kept Fertile.—Nitrogen is one of the elements of which plants use large quantities for food, and after the original amount that the soil contains has been exhausted, it must be replaced or the crop will fail. Now there are a number of ways by which this can be done, as, for instance, by rotating the crops, planting clover, or other leguminous crops, and using fertilizers.

The Rotation of Crops.—In the early days of farming it was found that where a crop of wheat was planted in the same field year after year the soil soon lost its productive power, though the reason it did so was probably not known. Later it was learned that if two very different crops were planted alternately both grew to much better advantage and this scheme of planting was called a *two year rotation*. Further experiment showed that when three different kinds of crops were planted in succession still better results were had, and this was known as a *three year rotation*, and, finally, it was found that when wheat, turnips, barley and clover were planted one after the other the soil produced good crops of each of them; this is known as the *Norfolk*, or *four year rotation*, and is widely used in all farming countries.

The Fixation of Nitrogen by Bacteria.—The rotation of crops is based on the fact that wheat and other cereals take the nitrogen from the soil, while clover, cow-peas and the like give it back to the soil. The way these plants and other legumes produce nitrogen is thus: On their roots grow *tubercles*, or *nodules*, that is, little swellings, formed of *bacteria*, a kind of living organism so small that to see one of them you would have to use a high-power microscope. Now these bacteria do not harm the plants and they have the very good quality of being able to take the nitrogen that is in the air and *fix* it, that is, they make it combine with sodium, or other elements, and so form soluble nitrates. When the plants die the fixed nitrogen remains behind in the soil where it is ready to be used by the next crop of cereals.

Natural and Artificial Fertilizers.—While the scheme of rotating the crops is of great value in keeping up the nitrogen and other elements of the soil that are needed to make plants grow, still it does not provide a large enough quantity of any of them to secure the best results. This is why *fertilizers*, that is substances which contain nitrogen, phosphates and potash, are so largely used. A good fertilizer is one that contains all of the above substances in such a state that they can be easily dissolved out by the water in the soil, and, therefore, can be readily assimilated by plants for food.

There are two chief kinds of fertilizers, and these are *natural fertilizers*, that is those that are the by-product of animals and other natural sources, and *artificial fertilizers*, or those that are manufactured for the purpose. Of the natural fertilizers barnyard manure was the first to be used, and as it is rich in nitrogen it is very valuable. Not only is it a good fertilizer, but when it is mixed with the soil, the vegetable matter in it keeps the particles of the soil separated and this allows the air to circulate freely through it.

Another kind of natural manure that is extensively used is *guano;* this is the excrement of seabirds that lived on the coast of Peru in South America, and with which is mixed the dead bodies of the birds themselves and the remains of fish on which they fed. Because guano contains nitrogen, phosphates and potash—the three chief foods required by plants—it is called a *complete fertilizer.* It was first used in England about the beginning of 1800 and in the United States a quarter of a

SHIPPING NITRATES FROM CHILE

Huge heaps of pure nitrates ready for bagging, and resembling snow drifts, at one of the largest Chilean plants.

century later. The guano deposits of Peru are enormous, and while twenty million tons have already been taken out, there is a bed of it left that is thirty feet thick.

Dry ground fish, or *fish scrap*, as it is called, is also used as a fertilizer for soils where the nitrogen has been exhausted. Every year enormous amounts of a kind of fish, called *porgy*, or menhaden, are caught to make fish-oil. Formerly after the oil was pressed out of the fish their bodies were thrown away, but later it was discovered that they contained nearly ten per cent of nitrogen. A new industry immediately sprang into existence and the remains of the fish which were discarded as waste were now dried out and ground up into a meal and sold as a fertilizer under the name of *dry fish scrap*. Some of the dried fish is treated with sulphuric acid, and this is sold under the name of *wet acid scrap*.

Of artificial fertilizers there are many kinds, so that every condition of soil can be taken care of and suitably enriched for the crop that is to be planted. Chief among these are fertilizers which contain large amounts of nitrogen. *Sodium nitrate*, or *Chili saltpeter*, is a compound brought from Chile in enormous quantities, and in its crude state it contains from two to five per cent of nitrogen.

It is then refined, when light-colored crystals are formed, and these often contain as high as fifteen per cent of *nitrogen*. Since it dissolves very easily in water it is readily absorbed by plants, and as it will make two blades of grass grow where only one would grow before, it is very much in demand as a fertilizer for lawns. In order to make it spread evenly it should be thoroughly mixed with twice its bulk of earth.

A nitrogenous fertilizer that is largely used is *ammonium sulphate.* When coal gas is made, it is passed through a solution of sulphuric acid, that is sulphuric acid and water, to rid it of the ammonia gas; the ammonia gas dissolves in the acidulated water and forms what is called *ammoniacal liquor,* and it is from this solution that ammonium sulphate is obtained. This salt has a grayish-yellow color and contains nearly twenty per cent of nitrogen.

In the early days of gas lighting, ammonium sulphate was considered a mere by-product, but when the chemistry of the soil came to be a recognized factor in farming, because of its high nitrogen content, it took its place as an important fertilizing compound. And not only is it used as a fertilizer but also as the basis of making, that is the beginning, of a large number of ammonium compounds.

The very latest nitrogen fertilizer is *calcium cyanamid,* or *cyanamid,* as it is called for short, or *lime-nitrogen,* or *nitrolim,* as it is often called. The making of cyanamid is another process for drawing nitrogen from the air.

Not more than ten years ago motor-cars were equipped with *acetylene gas* lighting apparatus. To make acetylene gas, water was allowed to drip slowly on a compound called *calcium carbide.* This compound is an electric furnace product and it was discovered by

Caro and Franke in 1895; the process of making it will be described in the chapter on *Electric Furnace Products*, which you will find further on. It is enough here to say that when a stream of nitrogen obtained from the air is blown across a bed of red-hot calcium carbide, they will combine chemically and form *calcium cyanamid* and *carbon*.

The calcium cyanamid contains one molecule of calcium carbide and two molecules of nitrogen, so you can see that cyanamid is rich in nitrogen. The cyanamid thus obtained, however, contains too many other substances to be used as a fertilizer and these must be removed from it before it is mixed with the soil. Among the impurities are *carbides*, *phosphates*, and *sulphides*, and when the air and the water of the soil react on these they set free gases which are very harmful to growing plants. These impurities are removed by a refining process, when the cyanamid can be safely used. But even then the nitrogen in it is not immediately dissolved by the water in the soil as is sodium nitrate; instead, the process is slower and the nitrogen in it is first changed into other compounds of ammonium which are easily dissolved and can be absorbed by the plants for food.

The Phosphate Fertilizers.—*Phosphorus* is the strangest of all elements. The old alchemists knew how to make it and because it glows in the dark they nicknamed it the *son of Satan*. Long before it was supposed to have been discovered by Brandt in 1669, an Italian alchemist, Prince San Severo, treated human skulls with various acids and then burned them in a furnace. The product apparently burned for months without loss of weight and it gave forth a ghostly light. The Prince called it a *perpetual lamp*, and for a long time he would not divulge the secret as he intended his family vault to be the only one to be illumined by it. As bones are treated with sulphuric acid and calcined in the preparation of phosphorus at the present time, there is little doubt but that the Prince had hit upon the process of making it.

Now although phosphorus is very poisonous and its vapor causes terrible ulcerations of the human body, each grown person has nearly two pounds of it in his system, and this is enough to make several thousand friction matches. The human body also contains quite an amount of sulphur, but fortunately there is not enough of the latter element to start a fire. Phosphorus is so essential to the brain that many people eat fish on days other than Friday to make them brainy, and from this comes the ancient saying, "No phosphorus, no brains."

Compounds containing phosphorus are found in small amounts in rocks, and as these are broken up to form the land, it finds its way into the soil, where it is dissolved and absorbed by various plants and finally helps to build up grains such as wheat, corn and oats. Then when you eat bread, corn-cakes or oatmeal the phosphorus in them is taken into your body and helps to make your bones as well as your brains.

Fertilizers containing phosphorus are, therefore, quite as necessary to plant growth as is nitrogen. Since both rocks and bones contain phosphorus there are, naturally, two sources from which it can be obtained. Fertilizers made from the first are called *mineral phosphates*, and those made from the second are termed *animal phosphates*. The phosphorus in minerals is locked up in the form of *calcium phosphate* while that in bones is mixed with other compounds. Calcium phosphate is a salt and as it will not dissolve in water readily it must be treated with sulphuric acid before it is mixed with the soil. Mineral phosphates contain a very large percentage of phosphorus, while bone phosphates contain about two-thirds as much.

If you will turn back to the chapter on *Old Metals and New Alloys* you will find that when steel is made in a Bessemer converter, slag is left behind. This contains a compound of phosphorus that will dissolve in water and, different from mineral and animal phosphates, it can be used on the soil without being treated with acid. This kind of fertilizer is called *Thomas slag* or *phosphate slag*.

Since it takes a long time for the phosphoric acid in both mineral and animal phosphates to dissolve in the water of the soil, both kinds are often ground up and mixed with warm sulphuric acid; this treatment renders the phosphoric acid soluble and forms calcium sulphate which will not dissolve in water. These substances are not removed from the rock or bone but the whole mass is ground to a fine powder. Because of the ease with which the phosphoric acid is dissolved out by the water of the soil it is called *superphosphate fertilizer*.

The Potash Fertilizers.—The starting point of potash fertilizers is a compound of *potassium*, a silvery-white wonder metal, which is so soft it can be cut with a knife, and so light it will float on water. It likes oxygen so well that to keep them from uniting it must be placed in naphtha or some other oil which does not contain oxygen. Potassium compounds are contained in rocks everywhere and when these are broken up or worn away they go into the soil where they become food for plants, and it is from these that we get a small part of our supply of *potash*.

When the metal potassium and oxygen unite they form potash, and plants contain not only potash but *tartaric*, *oxalic*, and other acids. To get the potash out of plants the wood of the latter is burned, when the heat decomposes the wood, and the *carbon dioxide* combines with the *potassium oxide* and forms *potassium carbonate* and this is a part of the ashes that are left. The ashes are now dumped into a barrel, which has a hole in it near the bottom, and every day a bucket of water is poured into it; as this seeps through the ashes it dissolves out the potassium carbonate, or *potash* as it is called, and on reaching the hole the solution, which is now called *lye*, runs off into a bucket. This process is called *leaching*. Finally the lye is evaporated leaving crystals behind and these are potassium carbonate.

In the olden times when nearly everyone burned wood the above process produced practically all of the potash used, but about fifty years ago great beds of potash were opened up at Stassfurt, Germany, and practically all of the world's supply of the salt has since come from this source. The potash deposits of Stassfurt were formed by the sea water which at one time flowed and ebbed over the district where the potash beds now are. The potash came into the sea, along with other salts, by the breaking up of the rocks which originally contained it, and as the sea washed forth and back it formed layer after layer of potash and so built up the enormous beds which are now being worked.

There are two kinds of potash salts that are used for fertilizing purposes, and these are *potassium chloride* and *potassium sulphate*. The crude potassium chloride is generally called *murate of potash* when sold as a fertilizer, while the common name of potassium sulphate is *sulphate of potassium*. In using these potash fertilizers care must be taken not to put the chloride on the soil where potatoes, tobacco or sugar beets are to be grown, for it hinders instead of helps them. The sulphate, while more expensive, is not harmful to crops of any kind.

CHAPTER IX

CHEMISTRY OF EVERY-DAY THINGS

It is curious how little the average person knows about the things he eats, wears and uses. Take, for instance, the commodity we call *sugar*. He knows that it is sweet and will sweeten his beverages and edibles; that the price of it was twenty-seven cents a pound during the war, that it is five or six cents a pound now, and that our chief supply comes from Cuba. But when it comes to the manufacture and chemistry of it he is often completely in the dark; and thus it is with many other common substances. So let us find out a little about a few of the most important of them.

About Cane Sugar.—There are various kinds of sweet substances which go by the common name of *sugar*, but that which we use for sweetening our tea and coffee, cereals, cakes, and many other drinkables and edibles is called *cane sugar*, or, to give it its chemical name, *sucrose*. Of course, cane sugar comes from cane, but *sucrose* also occurs in beets, sorghum, maple trees and in honey. Centuries before the Christian era the ancients had sugar cane and they also had honey, and as the sap of the cane and strained honey tasted very much alike, they called the former *honey of canes*. To give credit where it is due, the honey bees were the first makers of sugar, but as they mixed it up with other substances, it was not exactly suitable for sweetening things in general, and, again, they couldn't make it fast enough to supply the demand.

So sugar cane, which first grew in India, was cultivated there for many centuries for the sweet sap there was in it, but it was not until six or seven hundred years B.C., that the East Indian learned the knack of boiling it and making a syrup, or molasses, of it which would keep. Then it was that the sweet product of the cane became an article of trade, and it was used from that time on by all of the nations of the earth. But it took another fifteen hundred years before the human race learned how to make solid sugar out of the sap. When Columbus made his second voyage he took sugar cane from the Canary Islands to San Domingo, and from the latter place the plant was introduced into Cuba and other West Indian islands where the soil is particularly adapted for growing it. It also soon found its way into Mexico and Louisiana, and by the beginning of the seventeenth century the Old World depended almost entirely on the New World for its supply of sugar.

Sugar cane grows from six to twelve feet high and the stalks are a little larger across than a broom-handle. A crop is cut twice a year, then taken to the mills and *ground*, that is it is run between rollers which press every particle of sap out of the stalks. As soon as the sap is obtained a little *milk of lime* is added to it to prevent it from getting sour. The lime does this by throwing down the acids that are in it and separating the albumens out of it. The lime is then gotten rid of by precipitating it, in turn, with *carbon dioxide*. The solid matter that is thus thrown down, or precipitated, is removed from the sugar solution by filtering it in a press.

The purified sugar sap is next poured into vacuum pans, that is pans from which the air is exhausted, and heated so that it boils at a temperature so low it cannot possibly burn. This boiling process causes the water to evaporate until a thick jelly results and when this is allowed to cool the sugar, which is of a brown color, crystallizes out of it and leaves molasses, which is called *mother-liquor*, behind. The brown sugar is then placed in a *centrifugal machine*[8] which thoroughly dries it out.

The next step is to *refine* the sugar, that is to change it into white sugar suitable for table use. This is done by first dissolving the brown sugar in water, then filtering it through twilled cotton goods to get rid of the coarser impurities, and second, filtering it through a thick layer of animal charcoal, or bone-black, which removes the brown color and finally leaves a clear sugar solution.

This solution is evaporated in vacuum pans, and when it is sufficiently concentrated it is run into tanks where it is stirred until it crystallizes into white sugar. You have noticed that the crystals of sugar are sometimes fine and sometimes coarse; this difference

---

[8]A mechanical apparatus for drying out wool, yarns, etc., by placing them in a rapidly rotating shell which is perforated.

is due to and depends entirely on the length of time the sugar solution is stirred. While the table sugar we buy is perfectly white, the crystals of sugar have a yellow tint if poorly made. To make them white *ultramarine blue* is mixed with the sugar solution and this combines with the yellow element to make white, in exactly the same way that indigo combines with the yellow in cotton and linen goods when they are washed, to make them white.

IN A BEET SUGAR MILL

A big centrifugal machine in a Michigan mill, which separates the sugar in granular form from the molasses.

Away back in 1747, Marggraf, a German chemist, found that beets contained considerable *sucrose*. From the white beet he obtained a little over six per cent of sugar and from the red beet he got a little less than five per cent. Here, then, was a new source of sugar that would make the Old World independent of the New World for its supply, but it was fifty years after Marggraf's discovery ere sugar from beets was actually manufactured on a commercial scale. By this time sugar was in great demand, and the faster it was produced the more the world wanted of it, with the result that to-day sugar made from cane and sugar made from beets are running neck and neck in a wild race to supply enough to go around.

The first sugar to be extracted from the sap of the maple tree was the result of an experiment by a New England colonist in the year of 1752. While it is not a universal sweetening agent like sugar made from cane and beets, it certainly is good when eaten either as a candy or a syrup. The manufacture of maple sugar is carried on in the spring of the year wherever sugar maple trees grow, as that is the time when the sap rises and flows more freely.

About Camphor.—On the face of it *camphor* would not seem to be a very important substance, for about the only apparent use we make of it is to sprinkle it on our clothing to keep moths out and to use a dilute solution of it as a remedy for headache, colds, "flu," and the like; but as a matter of fact, it is employed in large quantities in making celluloid and for other industrial purposes.

Camphor as we know it is in the form of a gum which is really a solid essential oil. It is found in many plants but it can be extracted in commercial quantities only from the *Camphor Laurel*, a tree that flourishes in Japan, China and Formosa. There was a time, and that not more than a dozen years ago, when all the camphor we used was imported into this country from the Island of Formosa. For many years the entire camphor output of the Far East was controlled by the Japanese Government, and as the demand for the product grew greater with each succeeding year, the price of it was raised until it was so expensive as to be almost prohibitive. Then the chemists set to work to make it out of turpentine and other substances—that is *synthetically*, but this is another story which will be told later.

Natural camphor gum is made from camphor trees which are chopped down, cut up into small pieces and with the roots and leaves are distilled with water. As the vapors rise they are made to come in contact with and condense on rice straw and in this way the crude camphor gum is obtained. By distillation is meant that a liquid or a solid is changed into vapors by heat and the vapors are then cooled off, when they again take on a liquid or solid form. The crude camphor gum is refined, that is the impurities in it are gotten rid of, by *sublimation*, which means that the vapors are made to take on a solid form without liquifying first.

Camphor is a compound substance formed of carbon, hydrogen and oxygen ($C_{10}H_{16}O$). If you put some gum camphor into a bottle it will vaporize and form delicate crystals on the side of the glass on which the light shines. When water is added to spirits of *camphor*, which is made by dissolving gum camphor in alcohol, the camphor will be precipitated, that is thrown down in a fine powder. If you have ever tried to powder camphor you know that it is not an easy thing to do, but if you moisten it with a few drops of alcohol you can do so very easily.

Now here is a simple and very curious experiment: Pour some clean water into a soup plate, throw a few pieces of camphor into it and light them. As each piece burns, forces act on it which make it rotate and gyrate in a very strange and erratic manner.

About Celluloid and Pyralin.—In the chapter on *From Gunpowder to TNT* we explained what *nitrocellulose*, or pyroxylin, as it used to be called, is, or to give it its common name, *guncotton*. Now when guncotton is dissolved in a mixture of ether and alcohol a syrupy liquid results that is called *collodion*. In the old days of wet-plate photography the glass plates were coated with collodion just before they were made sensitive to the light by immersing them in a silver solution. Collodion is still used in photography, but instead of pouring it on a glass plate it is made into thin sheets which will not break, by pouring it on slabs and letting the ether evaporate. The sheets are then coated with a silver emulsion that is sensitive to light.

Now when guncotton and gum camphor are chemically combined they form a hard, white explosive substance that is not used for farm blasting or again for military guns, but for making all manner of useful objects that have very much the appearance of ivory but which is finer grained and, in some respects, more beautiful. Since celluloid is explosive, if a lighted match or other flame comes in contact with an object made of this compound, it will burn up in a flash. The danger of celluloid objects going up in smoke has been removed in the product sold under the trade name of *pyralin*, and this compound is now made up into the most beautiful toilet sets that the art of the designer and the skill of the manufacturer have yet produced.

While celluloid is really a present-day product in that it is only within the last few years that all manner of objects and articles have been made of it, it was discovered nearly sixty years ago. The story of its discovery is interesting, as is the story of all other inventions and discoveries.

The first efforts to produce celluloid were made by Alexander Parks, of England, in 1855. In his experiments to harden the dissolved guncotton to the proper degree he mixed it with many substances, including camphor, and to make the compound plastic, in order to be able to mold it, he mixed it with castor oil. The articles he made of it were called *parkesine*, but as both heat and cold had an untoward effect on them they were not a success, and after ten years of hard experimental work Parks gave up the attempt.

Working with Parks was a young man named Daniel Spill, who believing he could make a durable and temperature resisting product went to work on the problem. Finally he turned out a compound called *xylonite*, and while it was an improvement on *parkesine*, still it contained castor oil and so it had the same defects as *parkesine* though not to so great an extent. So ended the race for celluloid in England.

In the early sixties and for many years after, type was set by hand, and the typesetters used to put collodion on their fingers to prevent them from getting raw. When brushed over a surface collodion forms a thin elastic film, and you can buy it to-day for covering cuts on your fingers under the name of *New Skin*. Now it just so happened that John Wesley Hyatt, who was a typesetter during the Civil War period, intended to put some collodion on his fingers, when he found the bottle upset and its contents run out. Instead of a liquid or a viscous substance remaining, the ether had evaporated from it and left a sheet of solid material which in a way resembled ivory. Here was a compound that looked to young Hyatt as though it might be used for making billiard balls and other articles which had heretofore been made of costly ivory.

But alas and alack-a-day! when he tried to mold collodion he found that instead of expanding when it cooled, like iron or type-metal, it contracted to such an extent that it no longer bore a resemblance to the original object. Hyatt tried again (and if the truth were known he probably tried many hundreds of times) until, finally, he hit upon the secret of successfully combining guncotton and camphor without having first to dissolve them; this he did by simply heating them together in molds and applying pressure to them, when a third substance, which was finer in texture and more elastic than ivory, was produced and thus was born the remarkable product which we know as *celluloid*.

About Rubber.—This is a natural product but like celluloid it has made experimenters travel a long way. When Columbus made his second voyage to the New World he recorded the incident of seeing the natives of Haiti (Hispaniola) playing with rubber balls (though, of course, he did not use the word *rubber*, as this was a word of later coinage). Then in 1685 Juan de Torquemada, a traveller who had returned to Spain from Mexico, told of a tree he had seen in the latter country which yielded a sap (rubber) and of which the natives fashioned shoes. The first scientific record of rubber was made by La Condamine in 1736 who obtained some of it on a voyage up the Amazon River and on returning to France he presented samples of it to the French Academy.

La Condamine, or some other Frenchman, gave it the name of *caoutchouc* (pronounced *cu'-chuk*). This tough old name came from the word *caucho*, which was used in Brazil to mean a certain kind of rubber tree. Going farther back, *caucho* was derived from *caa*, which is the native word for wood and *o-chu* which is their way of saying *to weep*. Thus *caucho* in their language is literally a tree that weeps, by which they mean that rubber tears run out of it.

It was Joseph Priestley, a famous chemist of his day in England, who first called it *rubber*—a simple name that has stuck to it ever since, and this is the way it came about. He obtained some of it in 1770, and the only use he could find for it was to rub out lead pencil marks, and that it was a luxury in his time is shown by his statement that "its cost being three shillings (75 cents) for a cubical piece of about half-an-inch."

In 1823 Mackintosh, of Glasgow, Scotland, established a works where he made cloth waterproof by placing a layer of rubber between two layers of cloth, and *Mackintosh* is still a word to conjure with in wet weather. Then in 1825 rubber overshoes were imported from Para, Brazil, but they were next to useless, for they melted in summer and cracked in winter.

To make rubber durable in all kinds of weather was the goal many experimenters were striving for, but the efforts of all of them save one led to naught. Charles Goodyear, of Connecticut, was the lucky discoverer. The very year that he was born, that is in 1800, the first raw rubber was brought into the United States. He began experimenting with it when he was twenty-eight years old, and after ten years of laborious effort and poverty he finally hit upon the secret of making it elastic and durable.

He accidentally found that when rubber and sulphur were heated together a new compound resulted which was tougher and more elastic than the raw rubber and would neither get sticky nor crack under changing temperatures. This process of treating raw rubber when mixed with sulphur Goodyear called *vulcanization*. Further experimenting showed that by varying the amount of sulphur for a given quantity of raw rubber as well as subjecting these to different temperatures, rubber could be made very soft and elastic or exceedingly hard and brittle.

Rubber, that is raw rubber, is obtained by tapping rubber trees which grow abundantly in South America and Africa, when the sap runs out of them and is collected in cups. Rubber trees are tapped in different ways but the *spiral groove* method is one that is much in favor. In this method several spiral grooves are cut around the tree through the bark which provides the sap, and this then oozes out and runs to the bottom where it is caught. When the sap comes from the tree it is a white liquid about as thick as molasses, but it soon turns black and gets solid when it comes in contact with the air. As raw rubber is formed of carbon and hydrogen ($C_{10}H_{16}$) it is one of the *hydrocarbons*. When it is vulcanized, that is heated with sulphur, the compound takes on new properties and the formula then becomes $(C_{10}H_{16})_{10}S_2$). Raw rubber that has been mixed with the proper amount of sulphur for the particular purpose for which it is to be used, as, for instance, for rubber stamps, rubber shoes, or hard rubber for artificial teeth, can be bought already prepared, and it can then be placed in a mold and vulcanized.

CHAPTER X

CELLULOSE AND OTHER FIBERS

Textile Materials

CLOTH goods and fabrics in general are made of *fibers*, that is fine hair-like materials which are obtained from plants and animals. We get the fibers of plants that are used chiefly from *cotton* and *flax*, and the fibers of animals include those that we obtain almost wholly from *sheep* and *silkworms*. But there are also artificial vegetable fibers made, as well as imitation animal fibers, as you will presently see.

Cotton and Cotton Fibers.—While cotton did not provide the first covering for the nakedness of man, it is known to have been used in India and Egypt a thousand years before the beginning of the Christian era and fabrics were undoubtedly woven of it long, long before that time, and it is the most important fiber that we now have. There are several varieties of the cotton plant and all of these belong to the family that is known by the name of *gossypium*. It grows as a shrub and its leaves are dotted here and there with black spots. The flowers look something like those of the hollyhock which belongs to the same family; the flowers are of different colors but are usually white or pale yellow. The base of the flowers have purple spots on them and heart-shaped *bracts*[9] encircle them. As the plant matures, each flower on it changes to a round cellular ball, called a *boll*, and this is the fruit; it contains seeds and these are surrounded by beautiful soft hair-like fibers.

These cotton fibers are hollow and before the seeds get ripe they are filled with living cells, or *protoplasm*, as it is called. When the seeds ripen the protoplasm dries up and the fibers begin to flatten and twist, when the boll is forced open and the fibers are revealed; the cotton is then ready to be picked. The picking usually begins in August and often lasts up until December, or until frost comes. For this work everybody on the plantation who is old enough to be out of the cradle and young enough to be out of the grave is called on to help. Before the beginning of the nineteenth century the seeds had to be separated from the cotton, after it was picked, by hand, which was a very slow and tedious operation as a person could clean only about a pound of it a day. But in 1793 Eli Whitney invented the cotton gin and it not only does the work quickly but far better than it can be done by hand.

As the fibers have an elastic twist they are not only easy to spin but when spun they make a strong thread. The fibers vary in diameter from 1/600 to 1/1200 of

---

[9]These are modified leaves in flower clusters or subtending flowers.

an inch and are formed of cellulose. Since the cotton plant is a tender one it must be grown in a soil adapted to it and the climate must be warm and moist; these conditions are found in the Southern States, especially along the Atlantic and Gulf coasts, and the finest cotton comes from this part of the country. The two chief kinds of cotton raised down south are Sea Island and Egyptian cotton; Sea Island cotton is always pure and white, and Egyptian cotton has a slight yellowish color, and it is the latter that is used for balbriggan underwear, and other cotton garments.

What Cellulose Is.—Cellulose is a wonderful compound whose molecules are formed of six atoms of carbon, ten atoms of hydrogen and five atoms of oxygen. If you will take your knife and split the branch of a tree, or the stalk of a smaller plant, in two, and then look at it through a microscope of fair power you will see that it is built up of fibers, and around these are packed other compounds. Closer examination will show that the fibers are built up of cells and these are in turn formed of cellulose. It is these cells that give the plants their strength and rigidity.

Cellulose differs in various plants and in different parts of the same plant as far as its physical characteristics are concerned, but it always has the same chemical composition. For instance, in the bran of cereals it is so soft that you can digest it; in cotton and flax it is soft, long and hair-like; in elder-pith and cork it is short, light and springy; in the stalks of plants it is more or less soft and porous, while in trees it is harder and packed more closely together. The uses of cellulose are exceedingly diverse. In building houses, making furniture, weaving cloth, twisting rope, spinning thread, or pressing paper, the strength is due to the fibers.

These uses of cellulose are all old and well known, but in recent years it has been extensively employed in making nitrates, sulphates and benzoates and this is done by treating it with acids and various other compounds. When thus acted on, the composition of cellulose is usually changed, but in some cases it is merely dissolved and not decomposed; if such a cellulose mixture is further treated it results in a sticky compound whose consistency is about that of liquid glue.

Artificial Cotton.—Cellulose obtained from wood pulp is very cheap as against that of cotton, and by treating the former it can be made into threads, or *wood-pulp yarn* as it is called. A way to make a coarser yarn is to take narrow strips of paper that have been made from wood pulp and twist them. Such yarns are made into twine or woven into coarse fabrics which are used on walls and floors. A better fabric is made by weaving wood-pulp yarns with threads of cotton, flax and other plant fibers, and it is cheap and has good wearing qualities. These artificial cotton fabrics are sold under the trade names of *lincella, textitose, xylolin, silvalin,* etc.

Mercerized Cotton.—Ordinary cotton cloth that has been treated to give it a silky luster is known as *mercerized cotton.* It is so called after John Mercer, a calico-printer of Lancashire, who discovered how to make it in 1844. His process consists of treating ordinary cotton goods with a strong solution of caustic soda when it is changed into a compound known as *alkali cellulose*. The action of the soda on the goods makes it shrink about one-fourth of its original length. It is then stretched back, when the fibers are untwisted and made smooth which gives them a silky luster. The fabric is then washed when the fibers are changed into *cellulose hydrate* which makes them thicker and stronger than ordinary cotton.

Artificial Silks.—There are several kinds of artificial silk but all of them differ from artificial cotton in that the cellulose of the cotton is changed into a thick liquid, or viscous compound, which is then forced out of fine glass tubes with drawn points like the spinnerets of a silkworm when silk-like threads are produced. Artificial silk differs from real silk in that cellulose is a vegetable compound, and silk is an animal product. There are several distinct processes for making artificial silk but the chief ones yield *pyroxylin silk, cuprammonium silk,* and *viscose silk*.

Pyroxylin Silk.—In this process, which was invented by Count Hilaire de Chardonnet, the cotton is treated with nitric acid which changes it into *nitrocellulose*, that is guncotton. (See Chapter VII.) The guncotton is now dissolved in ether and alcohol when *collodion* results. (See Chapter XIII.) The collodion is then forced through little glass tubes whose jets are almost microscopic in size, and as the thread, or filament, comes forth the air causes the ether and alcohol to evaporate from it and a fine, smooth and lustrous thread is formed which is then wound on reels like silk from a cocoon. As these threads are highly inflammable they have to be treated with a solution of *ammonium sulphide* which extracts the nitrates that are in them and changes the nitrocellulose back into a compound that looks very much like real silk.

Cuprammonium Silk—In making this kind of silk, which is also called *Pauly's silk* after its inventor, the cellulose is dissolved in a solution of *cuprammonium*, that is a solution of *copper oxide* in *ammonia;* now when this solution has been neutralized by an acid the cellulose is precipitated, that is it is thrown down, in the form of a gelatin-like substance. This cellulose solution is then forced through glass jets, as described above, and the threads made to pass through a solution of dilute sulphuric acid; the acid gets rid of the copper in the thread which is again practically pure cellulose.

Viscose Silk.—Still another artificial silk is that produced by the *viscous process* which is due to Cross and Bevan. The viscous solution is made by treating cellulose with a strong solution of caustic soda when the fibers are *mercerized*, as described in the paragraph on *Mercerized Cotton*. The cellulose thus treated is then put into carbon disulphide, when a tawny-colored substance results, and when this is mixed with water it swells up like a sponge and then dissolves entirely. This liquid is now heated and a little acid is added to it, when a precipitate is thrown down which is cellulose, but this time it is in the form of a yielding, tremulous mass which goes by the name of *viscose*.

The viscose is then forced through glass tubes as

CELLULOSE AND OTHER FIBERS

before described, but instead of passing the threads through an acid solution they are suspended in a current of warm air in such a way that their own weight stretches them, and as they dry they are changed back into cellulose. While the sheen of cellulose silk is as great or greater than that of real silk and it dyes more easily than cotton, the chief fault to be found with it so far has been that it loses its strength when it gets wet, though when it dries again it seems as strong as ever. Viscose silk is the nearest approach to natural silk that has yet been produced as it has a luster that compares favorably with real silk and is nearly as strong. The greatest difficulty lies in its manufacture, as it is next to impossible to get the thread as fine as that produced by the silkworm.

Flax and Linen Fibers.—The fibers of the flax plant have been used for weaving goods so long, that the records of it go back to prehistoric times and it is likely that it was the first of the vegetable fibers to be made into cloth. So ancient is the flax plant that the stems and seeds of it have been found in the Swiss pile dwellings, and the woven goods of flax fibers have been discovered in the stone age remains of northern Italy. Long before the pyramids were built the Egyptians had learned how to make linen as fine as any we have to-day and they held it sacred. The priests were allowed to wear only linen robes when in the temples, and the dead were carefully wrapped in it, as an examination of mummies that are over four thousand years old clearly proves.

Linen fibers are obtained from the inner bark of the flax and so that the fibers may be as long as possible the flax is pulled up by the roots; the next step is to remove the seed and this is done with a rippling comb, hence it is called *rippling*. The stalks are softened, so that the outer bark of the stalks can be taken off, and this is done by *retting* them, that is either spreading the flax on the grass and letting it rot there, or else putting it in wooden vats and steeping it with warm water. This done, the rotted stems are subjected to *breaking* which breaks the decayed outer bark apart from the fibers when the latter are divided into shreds by *heckling*, or *scutching*, and these are laid parallel with each other.

The flax fibers are next bleached upon the grass and then they are boiled in lye which removes all of the coloring matter in them and makes them more or less white. After the flax plant has passed through the above processes it is cleaned and combed and the fibers are separated, then spun in moist air and woven. In the olden days when there was no such thing as haste, linen was bleached by wetting, washing, bleaching on the grass, soaking and rinsing, and these operations were often repeated as many as thirty or forty times, all of which took several months. These operations are now performed in as many days by modern methods, but chemical bleaching greatly weakens the fibers.

Sheep and Wool Fibers.—The skins of animals provided the first clothing for mankind, and the wool of the sheep and other animals was used before linen and cotton had come into vogue among the *élite* of the barbarians for the same purpose. Long before prehistoric man began to cultivate the land he raised sheep. In those early days the sheep were covered with hair, as the *argali*[10] and *musmon*,[11] which are believed to be the progenitors of the sheep, go to show. As a matter of fact hair and wool are one and the same thing, the only difference being that hair is thick, harsh and often straight, while wool fibers are covered with minute scales which overlap each other like those on a fish, but they are, nevertheless, very soft and generally curly.

When sheep lived in their natural wild state they were covered with hair but close to the skin there grew shorter hair that was soft and curly and which was wool. Then when primitive man began to bring various animals in to share his home with him he protected the sheep against the weather; the result was that the animals lost their long hair and the short fleecy wool grew longer and took its place. As civilization marched on apace, man greatly improved the quality of the fleece by selection and breeding and the wool that is now used is fine, soft, long and lustrous.

If you will examine a wool fiber under a microscope you will see that, like plant fibers, it is hollow and that it has a peculiar twist in it which makes it curl. This curliness is an important factor in spinning it into thread and because of it a single pound will make almost a hundred miles of thread. Wool fibers are made

---

[10]The argali is an Asiatic wild sheep of stout build and large and thick horns curved spirally outward.

[11]The musmon, or mouflon, is a wild sheep of the mountains of Corsica and Sardinia with very large and curved horns. It is believed to be a survival of the original stock from which the domestic sheep was evolved. It is covered with hair and not wool.

up largely of nitrogen, like *proteins*, that is albuminous substances, but unlike the latter it contains sulphur. After the sheep are sheared the wool is washed and two compounds are obtained from it; one of these is *suint*, or wool-perspiration, which dissolves in water, and the other is *yolk*, or wool-fat, which dissolves in benzine and ether. *Lanolin*, which will absorb its own weight of water, is pure wool-fat, that is, all of the impurities have been removed from it. It is largely used for salves and ointments. No imitation wool fibers have yet been made and neither have they been produced synthetically or otherwise.

The Silkworm and Silk Fibers.—Silk is a fiber that was evidently not known to the prehistoric races and even after man had advanced to a stage of civilization he seems not to have used it to any great extent. Silk came originally from China where it has been cultivated for more than four thousand years. The silkworm from which we get our silk is really a caterpillar that is hatched from the eggs of a moth called the *Bombyx mori*, or silkworm moth. This caterpillar has two glands which run along the inside part of its body and end in its mouth in two small openings, or jets, called *spinnerets*. It is from these glands that the silk substance, or *silk-glue* as it is called, which forms the fibers is forced out, and of which they make their cocoons.

The life history of a silkworm moth is this: the female moth lays her eggs, which have a blue tint and are about the size of the head of a pin, on the leaf of the *white mulberry* tree, which is the silkworm's natural food. Soon after the female has laid her eggs she dies

CELLULOSE AND OTHER FIBERS

and the male does not live much longer. The eggs are laid during the latter part of June and there they remain until the following April at which time the mulberry leaves unfold. When the eggs hatch out the silkworms are about as long and fat as a maggot. Each little fellow grows very fast until it is full size which is about as large as an ordinary caterpillar.

Can a leopard change his spots? The answer is emphatically *no*, but a silkworm can and does shed its skin four times in its short life of as many weeks. Between these changes it is very hungry and eats heartily of the mulberry leaves, and just before it gets ready to shed its skin the last time it goes into a deep sleep. After it has shed its skin the fourth and last time it gets ready to spin its cocoon, the first step of which is to make a thin shell that is to protect it and its silk fibers which it spins round itself. In spinning the fiber the caterpillar moves its head freely around while the rear part of its body remains quite still. After the cocoon is complete, the silkworm changes into the *chrysalis* stage, and from this a baby moth finally emerges when a new cycle of life starts all over again.

In the silk industry, however, nearly all of the moths are destroyed by dipping the cocoons into warm water which kills them, and only a few are allowed to emerge, as these are for the purpose of laying eggs. After the cocoon is soaked in water the glue-like fibers become soft, when it is easy to wind them onto a reel. As they are reeled, from four to ten fibers are run together and these form two threads; then these are run together to make a single thread of *raw silk*. If you will look at a fiber of silk just as it is taken from a cocoon you will see that it is formed of two silk fibers joined together as they come from the spinnerets of the silkworm, and that these are smooth and solid. Like wool, these silk fibers are largely formed of nitrogen, but unlike wool they contain no sulphur. Each fiber of the cocoon is from 2,500 to 3,000 feet in length and so silk as it is made by these little workers is not at all costly.

Paper Making

The chief ingredient of paper is cellulose, and as this is found in all plant life, almost any plants can be used for making paper.

Linen Rag Paper.—The best paper that can be manufactured is made from linen rags as these are pure cellulose and flax fibers are very soft and tough. The first step is to clean them so that no dust or other foreign matter will remain in them. They are then bleached in a hot solution of bleaching powder, that is chloride of lime, for about twelve hours, and then passed into a pulp machine; this consists of a cylinder fitted with rings of very sharp knife blades which set in a circular trough of water. The knife blades cut the rags into bits and these are washed in running water for six hours or so, when at the end of this time they form a pulp that is as smooth and even as heavy cream.

The pulp is now tinted with coloring matter, and then enough water is added to it to make it about as thick as milk. It is now strained to remove all of the

CELLULOSE AND OTHER FIBERS

lumpy particles and then it is spread on a slowly moving wire gauze belt that runs over a pair of cylinders which are some fifteen feet apart; as the gauze belt moves along the water in the pulp drains off and it becomes more firm. It finally reaches a cylinder called a *dandy-roll*, and on this are either parallel wires, various letters or special designs and these are pressed into the damp paper; it is these that make the *water-marks* you see on nearly all good paper and much of it that is bad.

After this is done the paper, which is yet so wet that it would fall apart, is run between heavy rollers which press the water out of it; from these it runs between other rollers which are hot and these dry it out so that it will hold together, when it looks like thin blotting paper. Next it is run through a vat containing a solution of glue and alum, or *sizing* as it is called, and when it comes out it, is run between another set of hot rollers that *calender* it, that is that press and dry it out, when it is finished paper and ready to be cut into sheets.

Wood Pulp Paper.—When you read a book or a paper you would hardly think that the thin, soft, flexible pages were once a tree, but it is even so. After the tree is cut down, and this may be pine, spruce, hemlock or other soft woods, the log is cut up into chips by a cutting machine. There are several processes used for converting the wood into pulp, and in one of them the chips are boiled in a strong solution of caustic soda under steam pressure. This breaks up the wood into cellulose and *lignin*, and the latter, which is of no value, is dissolved out. The pulp that remains consists of nearly pure cellulose and weighs about one-third as much as the wood of which it was made. The pulp is then thoroughly washed to get the soda out of it, and following this it is bleached by chloride of lime or some other compound or process which will set the chlorine free. The pulp is then made into paper by a similar process to the one for rag paper, described above.

A PAPER PULP MILL

The logs in the foreground are passed through machines which grind them into fine shreds for use in making paper.

CHAPTER XI

COLORS, PIGMENTS, AND PAINTS

PAINTS are used for three different purposes and these are: *first*, to please the eye, *second*, to prevent things from rotting or rusting, and *third*, to make wood and metal surfaces sanitary. The first *modern man*, that is the original man from which all of the present races came, was the first painter. He was a cave dweller and in Southern France at a place called Cro-Magnon and in Northern Spain, at Altamira, are caves, or rather caverns, which were used by successive generations for thousands of years for homes before houses were known.

The walls of these caves are covered with paintings of the animals that lived in that age and while the men who made them knew nothing of drawing in perspective, the paintings are, nevertheless, quite lifelike and possess real merit. When civilization had reached a stage where wood and metals were used in making various objects and in the construction of buildings it was soon found that wood had a tendency to rot away, and metal to rust to pieces. To prevent this, various kinds of coloring matter, obtained chiefly from the earth, were mixed with oil and when the resulting paint was smeared on the surface of things, air and water had no immediate effect upon them. In recent years the value of paints and varnishes for covering exposed surfaces, both outside and in, has been fully appreciated and there is a special kind of paint now made for every purpose.

About Paints in General.—Paints can be divided into two general classes, and these are *water colors*, that is paints made by mixing *pigments*, as the coloring matter is called, with water; and *oil paints*, that is paints made by mixing pigments with oil. Both kinds of paints are used for art work and for commercial work, the only difference between them being that for painting pictures the finest materials only are used and these are prepared with the utmost care.

For buildings and the like, water colors are good only for the temporary protection of their surfaces, to make them sanitary or to improve their appearance. Water colors are usually made by dissolving a pigment of some kind in water or in *sizing*, which is a weak solution of glue. Thus *ordinary whitewash* is made by mixing *calcium hydroxide*, that is *slaked lime*, with water. Now when this is laid on a surface that is exposed to the air the carbon dioxide in the latter is absorbed by the lime and combines with it, when *calcium carbonate* is formed and which, when dry, is pure white. A whitewash that lasts longer than ordinary whitewash is known as *government whitewash*. It is made by slacking lime in warm water, adding a solution of common salt, a paste made of ground rice and a solution of glue in which

COLORS, PIGMENTS, AND PAINTS

some Spanish whiting has been dissolved. Enough hot water is then added to give it the proper consistency.

Water colors for art work are usually made by dissolving a pigment of some color in a weak solution of glue or casein, and when the water dries out, the particles of the pigment will be cemented together. *Calsomines* for interior work are for the most part made of chalk dissolved in a weak solution of glue and then adding a pigment of the desired color.

Oil paints have far greater lasting qualities than water colors and for this reason wherever paints are to be exposed to the weather this kind is always used. Oil paints are made up of three, four, and sometimes five, compounds and these are a *vegetable oil*, a *pigment*, and a *volatile oil*; very often a *drier* is mixed in to make it dry more quickly and occasionally a *varnish* is added to make it glossy when dry. The reason vegetable oils, such as linseed oil or poppy oil, are used is that paints made of them harden by absorbing the oxygen of the air, whereas mineral oils harden by evaporation.

Oil of turpentine, or *turpentine* as it is called for short, is generally used to thin the paint, as it evaporates quickly after the paint is spread on the surface. Driers are often used to make the paint dry more quickly, and various compounds are employed; among these are *red lead, manganese oxide* and *cobaltic carbonate* and *nickel oxide* and *sulphate*. Varnishes are made by dissolving *lacs*, that is gums, in alcohol, or amber, copal, or other gums in boiled linseed oil. *Oil varnishes* are, of course, more permanent than *spirit varnishes* as the *alcohol varnishes* are called.

LINSEED OIL PRESSES
Presses at work in a big Sioux City plant.

What Pigments are Made of.—Pigments, as the coloring compounds used in paints are called, are obtained from several different sources and among them are: first, the natural pigments found in the earth and those obtained from plants and animals; second, pigments made by mixing or combining various substances; and third, those found in coal-tar products. In making paint a white pigment, such as *white lead* or *zinc oxide* is generally used as a base, and this is mixed with the oil first and then a pigment of the desired color is stirred in. These bases will be described presently.

Natural Pigments.—There are some *earth colors*, as natural pigments are called, which are either found in the natural state ready to use, or have to be treated by various processes before they can be used. Iron rust, that is *ferric oxide* forms several pigments of various colors.

COLORS, PIGMENTS, AND PAINTS

Red ochre and *yellow ochre* consist chiefly of ferric oxide; when this is mixed with *calcium sulphate*, it makes *Indian red*, and when mixed with *aluminum silicate*, that is *kaolin*, which is a kind of fine clay, it makes *Venetian red*. When yellow ochre is highly heated it changes to a rich brown color and then it is called *sienna*.

Raw umber and *burnt umber* are also formed chiefly of *ferric oxide*; raw umber has an olive brown color and this is due to the *silicon* and *manganese dioxide* in it; when it is heated to a high temperature the iron in it is changed to *hydrated ferric oxide*; it then takes on a reddish color when it is called burnt umber. A bright green pigment known as *terre verte*, or *green earth*, is composed of ferric oxide and *silicon oxide*, that is *silica*. The pigment called *van-dyke brown* was formerly obtained from the earth but it is now made by mixing ferric oxide, yellow ochre and burnt cork. *Barytes*, whose formula is $BaSO_4$, that is *barium, sulphur,* and *oxygen*, is the common name for *barium sulphate*, and is found in nature as *barite*, or heavy spar, and is treated with sulphuric acid to get rid of the iron in it. It is a white pigment and is often used to adulterate white lead and zinc white. It is also prepared chemically when it is known as *permanent white*.

Of the pigments that are produced by plants may be mentioned *indigo, madder, tumeric,* and *logwood*, but all of these are now made as good or better from *coal-tar* by synthesis (see Chapter XV), while *carmine*, which is obtained by drying the female *cochineal*, an insect that lives upon a kind of cactus in Central America, is also reproduced from coal-tar.

Chemical Pigments.—Among the chemical pigments, that is pigments which are made by combining elements or compounds, is *white lead* which is a basic lead compound. There are several different ways of making it, the chief ones being the Dutch, French and English processes. The Dutch process is the oldest, most primitive and the best but it is slow. In this process the lead is wound in spirals and placed in earthenware pots with some vinegar in the bottom of them. These are set in beds of horse manure, the decomposition of which gives off *carbon dioxide* and the heat generated starts the action on the lead. This forms a *basic acetate of lead* when a *basic carbonate of lead*, which is *white lead*, is thrown down. The English method is a modification of the Dutch method. The French method is more up-to-date as the carbon dioxide is obtained by burning coke. To make paint of white lead it is ground in oil and then thinned down with linseed oil and turpentine, and colored with other pigments. *American vermilion, minium* or *red lead*, as it is variously called, is made by gently heating *lead oxide* when it absorbs oxygen from the air and this makes it take on a bright red color. It is largely used for painting iron work.

Lead chromes are very lasting pigments but they are not at all cheap. *Lead chromate* is found in nature, and when *lead salt* is treated with a solution of a chromate, a bright yellow precipitate is thrown down, and this is the pigment called *chrome yellow*. Another lead pigment is *chrome red*, or *American vermilion*, as it is called, and this is a *basic lead chromate*. Then there are two kinds of *chrome green*, the first of which is made of

COLORS, PIGMENTS, AND PAINTS

lead chromate; and the second from *chromic oxide;* the latter pigment is a beautiful emerald green and is very permanent.

Because *zinc white* will cover a larger amount of surface, is cheaper and does not darken when exposed to the sun, it has been largely used in recent years in the place of white lead. It does not, however, last as well. Zinc white used to be called *Flores zinci*, that is flowers of zinc, and also *philosopher's wool*. It is simply zinc oxide and is made by either burning zinc in air, or heating *basic zinc carbonate*, which latter compound is made by adding *sodium carbonate* to a solution of *zinc sulphate*.

Prussian blue, which is *ferric ferrocyanide*, is a powerful pigment and is made by treating a solution of *ferrous sulphate* with *potassium ferrocyanide*, when a precipitate of a bluish white color is obtained. This is next treated with oxidizing agents, when a deep blue pigment results. A cheap imitation of Prussian blue is sold under the name of *Brunswick blue* and this is made by mixing a small quantity of Prussian blue with a large amount of barytes.

A wonderful blue pigment known as *ultramarine* was once made of the rare mineral *lapis lazuli*, which consists of *sodium* and *aluminium silicate* together with a sulphur compound. Ultramarine thus obtained was a very costly pigment; then in 1828 it was made by melting soda, sulphur and charcoal together. This was the first synthetic pigment ever made and it is even more beautiful than that obtained from lapis lazuli.

Further, there are now made a number of different colors of ultramarine, ranging from a deep blue to a sky blue and also white, red, yellow, green and violet. So the word *ultramarine* no longer stands exclusively for the blue color of the sea. *Cobalt* is a reddish-white metal and it is nearly always found in combination with *nickel*. *Cobalt blue* is a compound of *aluminium oxide* and *cobaltic oxide* and it is as beautiful a pigment as ultramarine blue.

A pigment that has the same formula as barytes ($BaSO_4$), that is it is *barium sulphate*, also goes under the name of *permanent white* and *blanc fixe*. It is made by the ton and is often used to adulterate white lead and zinc white, and also in making *lithopone*. This latter pigment, which is also sold under the trade names of *ponolith*, *oleum white*, etc., is made by mixing *barium sulphide* and *zinc sulphate* together, then heating them to redness and suddenly cooling the mixture in water, when a snow white pigment is produced. When lithopone is made into paint it will cover more surface than white lead but it is not as lasting and becomes discolored when it is exposed to the sun.

Black pigments generally wear well as they are formed chiefly of carbon. The pigment called *lamp-black* is obtained by collecting the soot of burning oils. This is a finely divided form of carbon that is deposited on a cold surface when placed in a flame. As oils are formed of carbon and hydrogen they are called *hydrocarbons*. *Bone-black* is made by charring bones, that is by heating them without enough air to allow them to burn up. The process is the same as that for making charcoal from wood and coke from coal. The pigment known as *ivory black* is the finest grade of *bone-black*.

How Lakes are Made.—There is an East Indian scale insect called the *Carteria lacca* and from it is obtained a beautiful scarlet and crimson pigment. The French word for *lacca* is *laque* and from this we get the word *lac* which means a gum and also *lake* which means a pigment. A *lake*, in the chemistry of paints, is formed when a color is made by combining a plant, animal or coal-tar color with the oxide of a metal. The metallic oxides that are generally used for this purpose are tin and aluminum, and when an organic color combines with one or the other of them a precipitate is thrown down and this forms a new pigment called a *lake*. Thus when *indigo* is combined with *aluminium oxide* a *blue lake* is formed; when *logwood* is combined with *aluminium oxide* a *purple lake* results; when *tumeric* is combined with *aluminium oxide* an *orange lake* is produced and when *cochineal* and *aluminium oxide* are combined that beautiful pigment known as *carmine lake* is obtained.

What is Meant by Vehicles.—The liquid that a pigment is mixed with to make a paint is called the *vehicle*. For mixing artists' colors *poppy oil*, which is a very fine and costly oil, is used. For all ordinary painting the pigment is mixed with *linseed oil*. This is made by grinding the seed of the *flax plant* into meal and then pressing it. If the flax seed is pressed when it is cold the oil will be very light in color, but if the meal is heated, much more oil can be extracted from it but it will be of a darker color; in either case it is called *raw linseed oil*.

When *raw linseed oil* is used to mix pigments with it dries slowly, and forms a film on the surface that is solid and yet elastic enough to stretch and contract with the surface which it covers. *Boiled linseed oil* is oil that has been heated and in which either *red lead* or *manganese dioxide* has been dissolved. As these compounds make the oil absorb the oxygen of the air faster, boiled oil makes paints dry quicker than raw oil.

Driers and How They Act.—To further hasten the process of making paints dry a special *drier* is mixed with them. By heating boiled linseed oil, which, as above said, contains red lead or manganese dioxide, until a syrupy liquid results and thinning it down with *benzine*[12] or *turpentine*, an *oil drier* as it is called, is produced. By melting *resins* with the oxides of various metals and thinning the mixture down with benzine or turpentine a *Japan drier* is made.

After the pigment is mixed with the oil it must be thinned down before it can be spread on the surface with a brush. Turpentine is generally used for this purpose and it is obtained by the destructive distillation of wood of pine trees or the pitch obtained from them. Varnishes are sometimes mixed with paints to make them glossy when dry, but they are more frequently

---

[12]There is a difference between *benzine* with an *i* and *benzene* with an *e* as the spelling indicates. Formerly the *benzine* that was used for cleaning was *benzole*, a volatile oil obtained from *benzoic acid*. Benzene as the word is now used, is *benzole* while *benzine* is obtained by the fractional distillation of *petroleum*, when gasoline runs off first, then benzine, and then kerosene.

used as a protective covering over paint and form a hard, transparent and glossy coat. A good varnish will not be affected by water, or dust when scratched; on the other hand a poor varnish is generally adulterated with resin, and when wet will become spotted and when scratched will break up into a fine white powder.

About Ready-Mixed Paints.—Time was and now is when a professional painter mixed his own paints, that is he would buy the white lead ground in oil, the pigments in their dry form, and the linseed oil in bulk, and mix them until he obtained the color, tint or shade he wanted. But there were many men, and women too, who wished to do a little painting on their own hook, but who were not skillful enough to mix paints which would live up to the color scheme they had in mind and, consequently, the results were often far from those they had fondly anticipated. To supply this "long felt want" ready-mixed paints were put on the market and they have proved a boon to the amateur painter.

The chief troubles with ready-mixed paints have been, first, that the white lead and other pigments in them would fall to the bottom of the cans, or other containers, and no amount of stirring would get them back to their original condition, and second, the paints were nearly always adulterated to the point of being useless. It was finally found that if a solution of *sodium silicate*, or *water-glass* as it is commonly called, was stirred into the mixed paint it would *emulsify* it, that is it would keep the particles of pigments evenly distributed throughout the paint. The water-glass, however, made them still less durable and so other *emulsifiers* were tried.

Among these were rubber solutions which are still used, but a simpler expedient is to mix a very small amount of water with them which holds the particles of pigments in suspension, and this scheme is very generally used. The tendency to use adulterants in mixed paints is growing less all the time, as the better makers of paints are fighting against the practice and some states have laws that regulate the quality of paints that may be sold.

CHAPTER XII

CHEMISTRY OF THE SUNBEAM

ALL life that exists, or has ever existed, on the earth is due to the action of unseen forces that are contained in the sun's rays. This may seem like a very sweeping statement but it is easily within the limits of proof to say definitely that if it were not for the kindly light and heat of the sun not only would plant life be impossible on our earth but animal life as well, and this, of course, includes human beings.

When seeds are planted they must be supplied with three things, besides a good soil, if they are to grow, and these are *moisture, oxygen,* and *heat.* If any one of these factors is missing the seeds will not germinate; for instance, if they have enough moisture and heat and the oxygen is lacking they will not sprout, and for this reason they should not be planted so deep that the air cannot reach them. Again if oxygen and heat are present and they are without moisture they will not sprout—which is a very clever provision of Nature for otherwise seeds could not be stored away for future use.

Lastly, seeds that have the proper amount of moisture and oxygen but which are not supplied with heat will not sprout, and so the heat must be furnished by the sun either directly or indirectly. If the heat is *artificial,* that is produced by some burning fuel like wood, coal or oil, or by an element heated by electricity the heat comes from the sun just the same for the wood is recent plant life, the coal is plant life that existed a million years or more ago, and the oil is formed of animal life that thrived when the world was young.

If the heat is set up by an electric current then the latter in turn is generated by either coal which is burned under a boiler or else by water falling on a *turbine*, that is a specially constructed water wheel. Where a fuel is burned to generate power it is produced by the action of the sun's rays, and where the power is generated by falling water again the sun developed it; this it did by evaporating the water from the lakes and oceans, when it ascended, and then on cooling it condensed into drops, fell to the earth and flowed down a river where it finally turned the water wheel.

The Laboratory of the Plants.—The green color of plants is due to the *chlorophyl* that is in them. It is a compound built up of carbon, hydrogen, oxygen, and magnesium, by the effect of sunlight. It performs two remarkable functions. First of all it colors them green—that is to say if there was no chlorophyl in them they would be white like mushrooms and toadstools which are devoid of it; and second, by means of it and the light of the sun, the carbon dioxide and water vapor absorbed from the air are changed into plant building tissues and other compounds, and oxygen is given off.

How the Sun Acts on Chlorophyl.—To show that the sun acts on the chlorophyl in the cells of a plant all you have to do is to place a very young plant that has grown from seed in a place where the light cannot reach it; now while it will keep on growing as long as the soil provides it with food it will take on a sickly white appearance. The way in which the carbon and hydrogen compounds, or *carbohydrates* as they are called, are formed in the cells of plants is passing strange as the following goes to show. The leaves of plants are provided with little openings, or holes, in the under sides of them and these are called *stomatæ* (plural of *stomata*). These are the nostrils of the plants and they breathe through them twenty-four hours a day, just as you and I breathe through our nostrils.

These openings, or stomatæ, are connected with tubes or ducts, which, in turn, lead to and end in the cells of the plants. Plants inhale the air and take the carbon dioxide from it; while animals exhale carbon dioxide, they exhale oxygen. It is from the carbon dioxide of the air that the carbon the plants need is obtained. When the carbon dioxide reaches the cells it combines with the water the plant has taken from the soil and together these produce *carbonic acid*.

Next the carbonic acid is decomposed by the action of the rays of sunlight working with the chlorophyl, and *formaldehyde* and oxygen are formed. It is at this stage that the plants exhale the oxygen. The formaldehyde, which is a gas with a stifling smell, is converted into *glucose*, or grape sugar, so called because it is the kind that is found in grapes. This sugar, which is only about one-fifth as sweet as cane sugar, is carried to various parts of plants where, on losing a molecule of water, two molecules of the grape sugar change into either *cellulose*, which forms the tissues of all plants, or *starch*, which is very closely related to sugar and to alcohol. Other compounds necessary to plant life are also made from the glucose.

Carbon Fixation by Sunlight.—What we call *sunlight* is made up of electric and magnetic forces linked together in the form of little waves which are given off by the sun. Plants must have sunlight in order for the cells to extract the carbon from the carbon dioxide or *fix* it as it is called. The energy of the light waves is not only necessary to help the chlorophyl get the oxygen out of the carbonic acid but it is also needed in forming starch and cellulose out of glucose.

While we have said that sunlight is necessary for plant growth, it is well known that artificial light, as that from an electric arc, which is white like that of the sun, will also serve the purpose, but again it must be remembered that the electric light is an indirect result of the sun's energy.

Action of the Sunbeam on Animals.—From what has gone before, it must be clear that plants can grow only with the aid of the light and heat from the sun, and it is just as true of animals, including man, as it is of plants. The herbivorous animals, that is those which live on plants only, are equally as dependent on the sun's rays as the plants they eat, though not as directly so. The carnivorous animals, that is those which eat flesh, are dependent on the herbivorous animals for their food and so they too could not live if it were not for the sun. Man is by habit both a herbivorous and a carnivorous animal but, curiously enough, when he gets a little civilized his stomach grows squeamish when it comes to eating carnivorous animals themselves.

How Light Acts on Chemicals.—While the action of light on plants and animals is wonderfully interesting still it cannot be easily seen; there are, however, various compounds that light acts on in a most striking manner, which are outside the realm of living matter, and these we can experiment with and examine with pleasure and profit.

Action of Light on Silver Compounds.—Light has not only the power of building up the tissues of plants and animals but it also has the power to decompose, that is to break down, certain compounds. The compounds that light acts on the quickest are those formed of silver, and among the most important of these are *silver nitrate, silver chloride, silver iodide,* and *silver bromide,* and all of these are or have been used in photography.

Silver nitrate is made by dissolving *silver* in a solution of nitric acid and water. When this solution is evaporated crystals of silver nitrate are formed. Then if the crystals are dissolved in water a solution is formed which the light will not affect as long as it is kept in a bottle, but if a little of it is brushed over a sheet of paper, or other *organic* surface, and exposed to the light it will instantly turn black. Owing to this action of light on silver nitrate it was formerly much used as a *hair dye* and for making *indelible ink*, but its chief use is for sensitizing plates and paper for photographic purposes.

The reason a solution of silver nitrate is not affected by the light when it is in a bottle, but is turned dark by the light when it is laid on collodion or paper, is by virtue of the fact that light acts on silver nitrate only when it is in contact with organic matter. By *organic matter* is meant a substance or a compound that is formed of matter that is living or which has once lived. Thus collodion is made of guncotton, which is made from the fibers of plants.

Silver chloride is made by dissolving *sodium chloride*, which is common table salt, in water and then dissolving some *silver nitrate* in this solution. The result is a *double decomposition*, as the chemists call it, which takes place thus:

| sodium chloride | plus | silver nitrate | yields | sodium nitrate | plus | silver chloride. |

The silver chloride is thrown down as a white curd-like salt. If, now, you will coat a sheet of paper with a solution of the silver chloride and expose it to the light you will see that it takes on a purple hue first and then changes to a brown color. It changed color because the light decomposed the silver chloride into *silver* and *chlorine*, the two elements which formed it, thus:

silver chloride plus *light* make *silver* plus *chlorine.*

As the latter is taken up by the paper or gelatin coating, all that is left on the paper is pure silver which has taken on a brown color.

Silver iodide and *silver bromide* are made in the same way as silver chloride and are acted on by the light in the same way but they are even more sensitive and, hence, are used for making rapid photographic plates and papers.

How Light Makes Photographs.—*The Daguerreotype*.—This process of photography is a very old one and was discovered by M. Daguerre, to whom the French Government gave a pension of six thousand francs a year (twelve hundred dollars). It consisted of a plate of silver, or a plate of copper coated with silver on one side, which was exposed to the vapors of iodine until silver iodide was formed on it. This operation had to be performed in a dark room lighted only by a dim yellow or red light.[13]

The plate thus prepared was placed in a holder and quickly taken to the camera where the operator inserted it and then drew out the slide. The *sitter* having already been posed and the camera focussed the cap of the lens was removed and the plate *exposed*. The rays of light reflected from the sitter onto the plate in the camera decomposed the silver iodide in proportion to their intensity, and this depended on the colors and the lights

---

[13] Red and yellow rays of light have far less effect on silver solutions than white light.

and shades of the original which formed the image.

If, then, the sitter wore white clothing all of the light that fell upon it would be reflected onto the plate, whereas if the dress or suit was black practically all of the light was absorbed by it and so none of it would reach the plate. In this way different colors and tints and shades reflected greater or lesser amounts of light which acted on the plate accordingly. After the exposure was made, the slide was again inserted in the holder when it was carried back to the dark-room and the plate removed. So far as the eye could see, the light had made no change in the sensitive film of the plate, but it had really decomposed the silver iodide.

The plate was next subjected to the vapor of mercury when it combined with the free silver and formed an *amalgam*.[14] The image which resulted gave very good values of the lights and shades, and to *fix* it, that is make it as permanent as possible, the plate was next treated with a solution of *sodium hyposulphite* which washed away that part of the silver iodide that the light had not decomposed. Finally a varnish made of *gold chloride* and *sodium hyposulphite* was poured over the plate, which was then warmed, when a positive picture resulted.

The Old Wet Plate Process.—Since only one picture at a time could be made by the daguerreotype process, other means were diligently sought for by which a number of duplicate pictures could be struck off. In 1831 Fox Talbot, of England, discovered a way to make

---

[14] An alloy or union of mercury with some other metal.

negatives of paper from which he could make as many prints as he wished. Since the grain of the paper negative was always shown in the prints made from it Sir John Herschel suggested the use of glass for the negative.

The old wet plate process consisted of first pouring upon a clear glass plate some *iodized collodion*, that is collodion to which was added some *ammonium iodide* and which when the ether evaporated left behind a thin transparent film. Next the plate was dipped into a bath of silver nitrate. The moment it was dipped, that is while it was still wet, it was put into a light-tight plate holder and the latter placed in the camera, and the exposure of the sitter was made. This done the plate was taken to the dark-room and *developed,* that is it was put in a tray and covered with a solution of *iron sulphate,* when the action of it on the silver compound of the film brought out the image, which, however, was reversed on the plate. When the image was fully brought out the action was checked by washing the plate in water. The next step was to fix the image so that the light would have no further action on the silver iodide. The fixing operation consisted of soaking the plate in a solution of *sodium hyposulphite*, or *hypo* as we now call it for short; this dissolved off the silver iodide which had not been acted on by the light. The plate, now called the *negative*, was washed in water, dried and given a coat of *amber varnish* to keep it from getting scratched.

From the negative, in which the lights and shades

were reversed, paper pictures were made, or *printed* as it is called. The sensitive paper was made by soaking paper in *sodium chloride*,[15] to fill up the pores and then coating it with a solution of silver nitrate. The negative was laid in a *printing frame* with the film side up and the silver paper was laid on top of the negative with its film side down, when the frame was set out so that the sun's rays would shine through the negative and on to the paper.

When the print was dark enough it was taken out of the frame and placed in a *toning bath* made of *gold chloride* and sodium bicarbonate dissolved in water. The purpose of toning the prints was to give them a richer color than could be obtained without it. Next the print was fixed in a *hypo* solution which dissolved the silver chloride that had not been decomposed by the sun's rays; it was then washed in running water to get out all the *hypo* and, finally, it was dried and mounted on a card.

The Modern Dry Plate Process.—The next big advance in photography was the use of the *dry plate* for the *wet plate*. The first dry plates were made by Scott Archer, of England, in 1851, and these he coated with collodion, dipped them in a silver bath and let them dry, but they were slow and unsatisfactory in general. In 1871 Maddox, of England, got up the *gelatine emulsion* process, that is he made an *emulsion*,[16] by heating silver

---

[15] A later improvement was to coat the surface of the paper with albumen, which gave it a glossy surface.

[16] A liquid or viscous substance in which fats or resins are held in suspension in minute globules. Milk is an emulsion in

nitrate and gelatine slowly together, coating the plates with it and letting them dry. These plates were not at all fast but they formed the basis for improvements which have resulted in plates so quick in action that an exposure of only one one-thousandth of a second, or less, will impress an image on the plate.

Different from a wet plate which must be used before it dries, a dry plate can be used any time. It is exposed in a camera in the way already described, except that a *shutter* must be used to make the exposure, as the cap scheme is altogether too slow. Dry plates are developed in a solution of *pyrogallic acid* or some of the newer developers like *metol* or *hydroquinone*. The developer changes the *silver bromide* which was acted on by the light into metallic silver and the parts on which the light has not acted remain silver bromide. A more recent improvement on the glass dry plate is the use of *celluloid films*, which make it possible to use hand cameras and *moving picture* cameras and projectors.

Velox Printing Paper.—Styles in clothing change from season to season, and likewise do they change in photographic papers though not so often. Silver paper, as just stated above, must be exposed to the direct rays of the sunlight and the toning, fixing, and other processes necessary to make them works of art require much time and manipulation. Besides, everybody got tired of seeing the same old brown and white pictures. So Dr. Baekeland, the inventor of *bakelite*, a cheap substitute

---

that the butter fat is so divided and suspended in it. A gelatine emulsion is gelatine which holds finely divided silver bromide in suspension in it.

for hard rubber, got up a paper in 1893 that had a silver emulsion coating on it like that used for dry plates, but on which the light acted very much slower, so that it could be printed by artificial light. Also like a dry plate this paper, to which the trade name of *velox* was given, is developed to bring out the image; it is then fixed with *hypo* and dried, when a beautiful black and white picture results.

Color Photography.—If you have ever looked at an image on the ground glass screen of a camera you must have been struck with the vivid beauty of its coloring. So has everyone who ever saw it, and so from the earliest days of photography investigators have striven to fix the image in its natural colors. The first scheme by which the image of an object could be shown in natural colors was invented by Frederick E. Ives, of Philadelphia, and it is known as the Ives *three-color process*. It begins by assuming that white light, as from the sun or an electric arc, is made up of three primary colors, red, green and blue-violet, and that all other colors, tints and shades can be produced by the proper blending of these colors.

A special camera is used which has three lenses in a row so that three separate negatives of an object can be made on an ordinary dry plate at the same time. Back of the first lens is a piece of red glass, back of the second is a green glass and back of the third is a blue-violet glass. These glasses are called *color screens*. The red glass lets only red light waves go through it, the green glass, green light waves, and the blue-violet glass blue-violet light waves, and screens out all other waves.

When the object is photographed through these color screens and the plate is developed, the image of the object made through the red glass is simply a record of all the red in the object, the one made through the green glass is a record of all the green in the object, and the one made through the blue-violet glass is a record of all the blue-violet light in the object. The negatives are without color themselves but they are *color records* of the object, just as a phonograph disk is without sound but is a *sound* record of the human voice or musical instrument.

From these three color records, or negatives, a positive lantern slide is made and this is placed in a kromskop[17] which has three lenses in it and back of one is a red glass, or color screen, back of the next is a green glass, and back of the third is a blue-violet glass. The lantern slide is now placed back of the colored screens and an electric light is passed through them so that the images of all three positives are projected on the screen where they are superimposed, that is made to exactly overlap each other. The picture that results stands out in natural colors precisely as they were in the object of which the photograph was made.

---

[17] A special magic lantern with triple lenses.

CHAPTER XIII

ELECTRO-CHEMICAL PROCESSES

Like light, electricity has a very decided action on certain chemical compounds and, the other way about, certain compounds produce not only light but electricity as well. The science of chemical reactions that set up electricity and of electricity acting on chemicals is called *electro-chemistry*. It began when Volta found in 1800 that a disk of zinc and one of copper separated by a piece of cloth dipped in vinegar produced a current of electricity.

Electro-chemistry may be divided into three general classes and these are, first, the production of electric currents by chemical processes, as with batteries; second, plating metal objects with metals of other kinds either to preserve them, to make them look better or for obtaining casts; and third, for extracting metals from their compounds and refining them. The processes for making synthetic and new compounds in the electric furnace is a secondary use of the current, for it is the heat of the arc light that works the changes and not the direct application of the current itself.

ELECTRO-CHEMICAL PROCESSES

How Electricity is Made.—There are several ways by which electricity can be generated and among these are: (1) *by friction*, as when a glass rod is rubbed with a piece of silk, when it is called *frictional*, or *static* electricity, (2) *by heat* acting on two unlike metals when it is called *thermo-electricity*, (3) *by chemical action* as when zinc and copper are acted on by a salt, alkaline or an acid solution as in an *electric cell*, or *voltaic cell* as it used to be called, and (4) *by electromagnetic induction*, as when parallel wires are made to cut through a magnetic field, as in the *dynamo electric machine*. The only process that concerns us here is the one by which a current is set up by chemical action.

Kinds of Electric Cells.—An electric cell is an apparatus for generating a current by chemical action, as stated above, and when two or more electric cells are coupled, that is joined together, they form a *battery*. Now electric cells may be divided into two general kinds, namely the *primary cell* and the *secondary cell*, or *accumulator* as it is called in England, or *storage cell* as we call it here in the States. The difference between them is that a primary cell generates a current by the direct chemical action of the solution, or *electrolyte* as it is called, on the zinc element in it, while a secondary cell must be *charged* by a current of electricity before it can deliver a current; the electricity, however, is not *stored up* in it as you will shortly see.

Primary Battery Cells and How They Work.—Now while all primary cells generate a current on the same principle they, likewise, are of two general kinds and these are the *dry cell* and the *wet cell*. The dry cell is not all dry, but is so called because it does not contain any free liquid and, further, it is sealed to prevent any possible chance of leakage. It is widely used for a variety of purposes such as flash-lamps, electric bells, annunciators and all places where a large but momentary current is needed.

The wet cell contains a liquid electrolyte, and some are made with alkalis and some with acids. These cells are again divided into *open circuit* cells and *closed circuit* cells. With a cell of the first kind the wires connected with it must be kept open, that is separated except for the brief interval the current is being used, while with the second, the circuit must be kept *closed* so that the current can flow through it all the time.

About Open-Circuit Cells.—All primary cells are made up of three parts besides the electrolyte, or solution, and some of them have four parts. The parts of a simple cell consist of a cup, or jar, that holds the electrolyte and in which are immersed a piece of zinc and a piece of carbon. These pieces are called *elements*, while the zinc is known as the *cathode* and the carbon element as the *anode*. It is important to remember these names for they are used altogether in the analysis of water, in electroplating and in the electrolysis of various compounds. Binding posts are usually fastened to the upper ends of the elements so that wires can be connected easily and quickly to them.

A *dry cell* consists of a can, or cup, made of sheet zinc and this forms the *negative* element, or cathode, of the cell. A carbon rod, which is the *positive* element,

ELECTRO-CHEMICAL PROCESSES

or anode, is set in the middle of the zinc cup, but does not touch it, and an electrolyte, which is an active paste, is filled in between the electrodes to within half-an-inch of the top, when melted pitch is poured over it and which, when cold, holds the carbon and the paste in place and prevents the possibility of any liquid from leaking out. The paste is made of *zinc oxide, zinc chloride, ammonium chloride,* which is *sal ammoniac, manganese dioxide,* and *plaster-of-paris,* all of which are mixed into a paste with water.

Now as long as the wires which are connected with the elements are kept apart, that is as long as the circuit remains *broken,* no chemical action will take place between the electrolyte and the zinc, but the moment the wires are joined together a current will be set up and flow through the electrolyte from the zinc to the carbon, and through the wire circuit from the carbon to the zinc. Since the current flows from the carbon to the wire connected with it, it is called the positive element, and since it flows from the wire to the zinc this is called the *negative* element.

A *wet cell,* which uses a solution of sal ammoniac for the electrolyte, comprises a glass jar, a carbon plate set into a porous cup,[18] with a compound made of manganese dioxide and powdered carbon packed around it; a zinc rod is then set in the jar and the latter filled with a solution of sal ammoniac dissolved in water. The chemical action of both the dry and the wet cells is the same as follows: When the circuit is closed the sal ammoniac acts on the zinc and forms *zinc chloride;* at

[18]This is made of unglazed earthenware like a flower-pot.

the same time it sets free both ammonia and hydrogen. The purpose of the manganese dioxide is to oxidize the hydrogen which it does slowly; if the circuit is kept closed for any length of time the hydrogen is set free faster than it is oxidized and this prevents further chemical action from taking place, when the cell is said to be *polarized*. On breaking the circuit and letting the cell stand for a short time, it recovers and will again generate a current.

About Closed Circuit Cells.—Different from the open circuit cells just described, closed circuit cells give more powerful currents and the circuit can be kept closed for long periods at a time. The *Bunsen cell* was invented by Professor Bunsen, of Germany, in 1841, and is one of the best of the closed circuit cells, hence it is good for electroplating on a small scale. It is made up of a glass jar in which there is a large cylinder of zinc; a porous cup sets inside of this and inside of the porous cup sets a carbon plate. Two different compounds are used for the electrolyte, the first being *concentrated nitric acid*, which is placed in the porous cup, and *dilute sulphuric acid* is placed in the glass jar. Now when the circuit is closed the action of the sulphuric acid on the zinc sets hydrogen free; this goes through the porous cup and on coming in contact with the nitric acid produces *nitrogen peroxide*, a very irritating and corrosive gas, which passes off from the cell.

The *gravity*, or *crowfoot*, cell is used on telegraph lines where a current from a dynamo is not available. It is a simplified form of a Daniell cell. As far back as 1836 Professor Daniell, of London, was working on a cell which would generate a constant current and he succeeded very well. His cell consisted of a glass jar in which there was placed a copper cylinder. Inside the latter was a porous cup and inside of this a zinc rod. The glass jar was filled with a saturated solution of *copper sulphate*, that is *blue vitriol*, and the porous cup was filled with a dilute solution of zinc sulphate; the porous cup allowed the two solutions to mix very slowly.

The gravity cell is really a Daniell cell without the porous cup. It consists of a glass jar with a star-shaped strip of copper resting on the bottom; the bare end of an insulated wire is soldered to the copper and this leads up to and outside of the jar, while a heavy zinc casting with finger-like projections is hooked on to the top of the jar. As the zinc looks something like a crow's foot the cell is often called a *crowfoot cell*. The copper star in the bottom of the jar is filled in with *copper sulphate* and a solution, made up of a very little *sulphuric acid* dissolved in water, is poured into the jar until it covers the zinc.

When the circuit of this cell is closed the sulphuric acid acts on the zinc and forms *zinc sulphate*, and as this is lighter than the copper sulphate, it remains on top of the latter solution; as the difference in the weight of the two solutions keeps them separated it is called a *gravity cell*. At the same time that zinc sulphate is formed on the zinc element, metallic copper is deposited on the copper element, and there is an increase of zinc sulphate that corresponds exactly to the loss of the copper sulphate.

Local Action in Cells.—The zinc that is used in cells

is never pure but contains particles of carbon, iron, etc.; now when an acid electrolyte is used, as in the Bunsen and gravity cells, a chemical action is set up between the impure particles and the zinc atoms. This gives rise to what is called *local action*, which means that each pair of these little couples act as the elements of a minute cell and set up a current. This action of the electrolyte eats the zinc away and at the same time it lessens the current output of the cell. To prevent this local action, Sturgeon, the British scientist who invented the electromagnet in 1832, washed the zinc with sulphuric acid and then rubbed mercury over its surfaces. This process, which is called *amalgamation*, because the zinc and mercury form an *amalgam*, brings the pure zinc to the surface and at the same time it covers the impure particles; it also forms a smooth, bright surface which soon becomes covered with a film of hydrogen and this protects the zinc except when the cell is in action.

Storage Battery Cells and How They Work.—While a primary cell generates a current by the chemical action of the electrolyte on the zinc element and, consequently, both the zinc and the electrolyte are used up, on the other hand the secondary, or storage, cell can deliver a current only after it is *charged* by passing a current through it that is generated by a dynamo or some other source of direct current. When this is done the storage cell will deliver practically the same amount of current as that which was used in charging it.

The first storage cell was made by Gaston Planté, of France, in 1860. His cell consisted of a pair of lead plates separated with a sheet of felt and all of which were rolled up together and then immersed in dilute sulphuric acid. This cell was at once simple and compact and it was efficient, too, but it had the great drawback of having to be charged and discharged many times before it would deliver anywhere nearly the same amount of current that was passed into it. The chemical action that took place in preparing the lead plates was this: A current was passed through the cell until one of the lead plates was changed into *lead peroxide* and the other one was changed into *spongy lead*. To save the time and current required for this operation Camille Faure, also of France, made the important improvement, twenty years later, of *pasting* a layer of lead peroxide to one of the lead plates and of spongy lead to the other plate. The trouble with the Faure cell was that the *active material*, as the lead peroxide and spongy lead is called, disintegrated, that is it broke up, not only by the chemical action but on being moved about.

Storage Cells of To-day.—There are two kinds of storage cells and these are the *lead cell* and the *nickel-steel cell*. A lead cell is made up of two elements called *grids;* both of these grids are formed of sheets of lead punched full of holes, or which have grooves cut in them. The positive grid is filled with lead peroxide, while those of the negative grid are filled with spongy lead, that is pure lead which is finely divided. Two or more positive grids are placed parallel with, but are separated from, each other by about half an inch and all are joined together at one end by a lead connection, called a *strap*, to which a terminal wire or cable can be attached. This bunch of grids is called the *positive group*.

Next, the same number of negative grids are connected together in the same way as the positive grids, and this is called the *negative group*. The two groups are then pushed together so that their grids alternate and to keep them apart thin boards, called *separators*, are slipped in between each pair, when the *element* is complete. The element is next set into a jar which contains an electrolyte made of sulphuric acid and water when the cell is ready for service.

However, before the cell can deliver a current it must be *charged*, and to do this its terminals must be connected to a dynamo or some other source of direct current. When a current flows into the cell a chemical action takes place which changes the spongy lead of the positive grid into lead peroxide, and the lead peroxide of the negative plate into spongy lead. To obtain a current from the cell all you need to do is to close the circuit when a chemical reaction takes place and the spongy lead of the negative grid changes back into lead peroxide, and the lead peroxide of the positive plate changes back to spongy lead. From this you will see that the charging current is not stored up in the cell, but that it sets up a chemical action between the electrolyte and the lead compounds so that when these again react on each other an electric current is produced. What is really stored up is chemical energy and not electricity.

ELECTRO-CHEMICAL PROCESSES

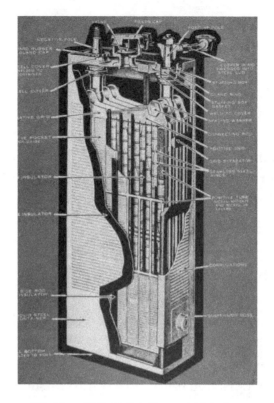

EDISON STORAGE BATTERY

An alkalkine cell constructed of steel, and weighing about half as much as a lead cell.

The Edison Storage Cell.—Because lead is heavy when compared with the same volume of other metals, and lead grids tend to disintegrate after long or hard service, Thomas A. Edison, the great inventor, spent many years and much money in making a storage cell which would be lighter for the same output and which would not wear out. The plates of the Edison cell are made of sheet *nickel-steel* with holes punched in them and in which the active material is held. The active material in the positive plates is *nickel peroxide* and in the negative plates it is *iron oxide*. All the positive plates are connected together in one group, and all of the negative plates are connected in another group, as in a lead cell; the two groups are then pushed together so that the positive and negative plates alternate, and a sheet of hard rubber is slipped between each pair to keep them apart; the element so formed is set in a jar which contains an *alkaline electrolyte* made by dissolving *caustic potash* in water.

When the cell is charged the current flowing into the electrolyte sets oxygen free and this acts on the nickel oxide and changes it to peroxide; at the same time where the current leaves the electrolyte, hydrogen is set free, and this changes the iron oxide to spongy iron. When the cell discharges, the action is reversed, the nickel peroxide is converted into nickel oxide and the spongy iron into iron oxide. The Edison cell takes up about the same amount of room as a lead cell of the same capacity but it weighs only about half as much.

Electroplating and Electrotyping.—The process of coating a cheap metal with a more costly metal by electricity is known as the *electro-deposition of metals*, or, in every-day language, as *electroplating*. To do electroplating you need a source of current and for experimental purposes you can use a Bunsen cell, or a gravity cell will do. You will also need a large jar, a plating solution, a couple of copper rods, an *anode*, that is a piece of the pure metal you want to plate the object with, and finally, the object which you want to plate.

Now make a plating bath by dissolving some copper sulphate in water and put it into the jar.

This done, lay the copper rods across the top of the jar and then connect them to the elements of the cell. On the bar that is connected with the carbon element hang the copper anode, and on the bar connected with the zinc element hang the object to be plated; just before doing so dip it into a boiling solution of *sodium carbonate*, or just plain *soda*, as it is called, for it must be perfectly clean and free from grease. Now the copper sulphate solution contains positively charged particles of copper, and negatively charged sulphuric acid particles. When the current is turned on the positively charged copper particles are attracted to and deposited on the object to be plated suspended from a rod connected to the zinc element of the cell. For each copper particle that is deposited from the solution, a positively charged copper particle is passed from the copper anode to the solution, thus its strength is always the same.

When common type is set up and a large number of impressions are needed, an *electrotype* is generally made of it, for the type-metal[19] is so soft that the letters would soon lose their clear-cut edges. To make an electrotype, an impression is taken of the type that is set up with wax, and the latter is then brushed over with powdered graphite so that it will conduct a current of electricity. The wax impression is then hung in the plating bath and plated until a thin copper impression is formed

---

[19]Type-metal is an alloy formed of three parts of lead and one of antimony.

of it which is exactly like the original type. The wax is melted away and the copper impression is backed up with type-metal to make it thicker and stronger. Finally the plate is mounted on a wood block which will make it just type high, when the electrotype is finished and ready to be printed from.

In plating with gold the anode is, of course, made of pure gold and the bath is made of *gold chloride* and *sodium cyanide*, which is a very poisonous compound, dissolved in water; and then to make the gold cling more easily to the object to be plated the latter is *quicked*, that is it is dipped into *mercuric nitrate*. The bath for silver plating is made by dissolving *silver nitrate* and *potassium cyanide* in water. Plating with nickel is harder to do than plating with any of the above-named metals. The bath is made by dissolving *double sulphate of nickel* and *ammonium* and *ammonium sulphate* in water.

What Goes On in the Bath.—A plating bath of whatever kind is made up of a salt that is formed by combining a metal with an acid. Thus *copper sulphate* is formed of the metal copper and sulphuric acid. Now when this compound is dissolved in water to make the bath it is decomposed by the water, that is broken up, into a positive part, the metal, and a negative part, the acid portion. The positive metal is attracted to the cathode, which is the negative pole, and in electroplating is formed of the article to be plated, while the anode, which is the positive pole and made of pure metal, attracts the negative acid part, and there forms more of the copper sulphate. This is because salts are decomposed by water into an electro-positive, or metallic part, and an electro-negative, or non-metallic part.

The Hall Electrical Process.—The Hall apparatus consists of a large iron tank lined with carbon, and this forms one of the poles to which the source of current is attached, the cathode. The melted cryolite and *bauxite* is poured into the tank and a number of large carbon rods, which forms the other pole, the anode, and is connected to the source of the current, is lowered into the mixture. The current of electricity is then passed from the carbon poles to the carbon lining, and so goes through the mixture; the current decomposes the mixture when the aluminum falls to the bottom of the tank. To produce the aluminum as cheaply as possible the electricity is generated by water power, the American plant being located at Niagara Falls. By the Hall process aluminum can be produced for less than twenty cents per pound.

CHAPTER XIV

PRODUCTS OF SYNTHETIC CHEMISTRY

THE first chemical operation ever performed by man, other than taking something into his own system, was to separate the elements of wood, or some other fuel, of which it was made, by burning it, but the only thing he knew about the action was that it gave out light and heat. Now in chemistry when a compound is split up into its original elements the process is called *analysis*, and oppositely when certain elements are combined to form a compound the process is called *synthesis*.

The chemist who first burned fuel and was able to determine what the elements were that it was formed of made the first *qualitative*[20] *analysis*. The old alchemists mixed up various substances which often combined and produced new compounds but they didn't know what they were or why they were formed, but the chemist who first took two known elements and made them combine to form a compound he wanted was the first to perform the operation of *qualitative synthesis*.

---

[20]So called because the quality of it is found out, that is, what it contains.

PRODUCTS OF SYNTHETIC CHEMISTRY

What Natural, Artificial and Synthetic Compounds Are.—When two or more elements are combined by Nature the compound which results is, of course, a *natural* one. When two or more substances are mixed, or combined, by the hand of man so that the resulting compound imitates to some extent one that has been made by Nature the product is an *artificial* one. Many attempts have been made by chemists and others to make compounds which would have the properties and serve the purposes of the natural ones, but in nearly every case the artificial products were unsuccessful.

But there is another way, one that is more scientific and better in every respect for making substitutes of natural compounds and this is by *chemical synthesis*, that is the chemist combines the same elements, using the same atomic weights and molecular proportions of them that Nature does, when the resulting products will have exactly the same properties as the natural ones and therefore are identical with them. Compounds of this kind that are made by the chemist are called *synthetic products*.

How to Make Synthetic Water.—As a simple illustration of what is meant by a synthetic product you can make the experiment of forming water by means of the electric spark which was described in the second chapter. It is a good plan to analyze some water first by passing a current of electricity through it when it will be *decomposed*, that is separated into its two component gases, namely, hydrogen and oxygen; further, you will find that there will be twice the volume of hydrogen in one of the test-tubes that there will be of oxygen in the other test-tube, and this shows that there are two atoms of hydrogen to each atom of oxygen (H_2O) in each molecule of water formed. This, then, is the analysis of water.

Now take your *eudiometer*, which you will find described in Chapter II, and transfer the two gases which you have obtained by analysis into its tube, when they will simply form an explosive mixture; but what you want is to make them combine chemically, and to do this you need only to cause an electric spark to jump between the ends of the wires in the tube, and the gases will explode and combine and the result will be a small drop of clear liquid. This liquid is water and you will have produced it synthetically. It was by this experiment that Cavendish first showed the exact nature of water. Of course water is so plentiful there is no object in making it by synthesis except to prove that it is formed of hydrogen and oxygen, so the process remains a laboratory experiment.

Some Other Simple Compounds.—The value of being able to combine various elements so that they will form compounds that are identical with natural ones is to give us a cheaper or a more abundant supply of them than we can get from Nature's storehouse. Now it is a far easier matter to analyze a compound and find out exactly what elements it is formed of than it is to take the elements and make the same number of atoms of them combine to form the original compound.

Where only two elements are needed to make a compound, as *hydrogen* and *oxygen* to form water, *mercury* and *iodine* to form *mercuric iodide*, or *copper* and *sulphur* to form *copper sulphide*, the processes are easy and no skill is required to work them out, for a simple chemical action takes place; in the case of water this is produced by an electric spark; in mercuric sulphide by rubbing the elements together hard, and in copper sulphide by dipping copper into melted sulphur. But where a *reaction* between the elements of two compounds is required, that is where an element of the first compound must act on an element of the second compound and, oppositely, the other element of the second compound must act on the other element of the first compound, the difficulties of producing a desired synthetic compound are multiplied.

An Early Synthetic Compound.—Take, for instance, *potassium nitrate*, which is one of the chief ingredients of black gunpowder. Before the Crimean War broke out in 1825 potassium nitrate had been chiefly obtained from India, and there had always been enough to supply all the armies of the world. But when the war was on, France ran short of it and offered a prize to anyone who could make it.

Now there was a plentiful supply of *potassium chloride*, which looks very much like sodium chloride (common salt) and has about the same properties, and *sodium nitrate*, that is Chili saltpeter, so there was devised a method of making potassium nitrate from these. When strong solutions of potassium chloride and sodium nitrate were mixed together, the *reaction*, which is called *double decomposition,* yielded sodium chloride and potassium nitrate. Here is the way the reaction works out:

potassium chloride plus *sodium nitrate* make *sodium chloride* plus *potassium nitrate.*

This, then, was an early application of synthetic chemistry to supply the needs of war, and it was carried on to a remarkable extent by the various nations during the World War.

How Synthetic Camphor is Made.—You have read in Chapter VII that camphor is a gum made by chopping up and distilling the wood of the camphor tree and that for many years the Japanese government practically controlled the entire output of camphor and so was able to make it pay an enormous revenue. Now each camphor molecule consists of 10 atoms of carbon, 16 atoms of hydrogen and 1 atom of oxygen, or to write it as a formula, $C_{10}H_{16}O$. Camphor trees, as you know, do not grow in the United States but we have great forests of pine trees and these give us all the *turpentine* we want and to spare.

But what, you may ask, has turpentine to do with camphor? Just this, each molecule of turpentine is composed of 10 atoms of carbon and 16 atoms of hydrogen, or expressed in the shorthand of the chemist, $C_{10}H_{16}$. As you can see, the only difference between camphor and turpentine is that the former has one atom of oxygen to each molecule formed by the carbon and hydrogen atoms, whereas the latter has none. It must be clear now, if you can supply the extra atom of oxygen to the turpentine you will have produced camphor.

PRODUCTS OF SYNTHETIC CHEMISTRY

To make a given number of atoms combine with the molecules of certain other elements, and especially with the molecules of certain other compounds is often a hard thing to do but it can be done if you hit upon the right way to go about it and this is generally done by making a series of experiments.

Some twenty years ago Bradley and Lovejoy, two American chemists, tackled the problem and after long and continuous experimenting they worked out a process for making *synthetic camphor*. They started with *turpentine* and *oxalic acid*,[21] which latter is formed of 2 atoms of carbon, 2 atoms of hydrogen and 4 atoms of oxygen, ($C_2H_2O_4$). From this formula you will see that oxalic acid is formed of one-half oxygen by weight and since it is a vegetable acid, it probably gives up its oxygen more easily when it is acted upon by other vegetable compounds than it would if it were a mineral acid.

The turpentine and oxalic acid are put into a steam-heated vat, which is lined with asbestos to keep in the heat, and when this reaches a temperature around the boiling point they combine and form *pinol oxalate* and *pinol formate*, both oily liquids. Next *sodium hydroxide*, which is a *base*, is put into the vat and the steam is again turned on. In this last operation the oxygen atoms of the oxalic acid combine with the atoms of the carbon and hydrogen of the turpentine in the proper proportion, when camphor molecules result; the camphor thus

---

[21] Oxalic acid is largely made from sawdust which latter will yield more than half its weight of crystals of this salt.

made is crude and mixed up with various kinds of *aromatic oils*, that is heavy, sweet-smelling oils which are used for perfuming soaps and the like.

To separate the crude camphor, which is now called *borneol*, from the oils, the mass is *distilled*, that is it is heated until it vaporizes when the vapor is condensed. But there is more to the distillation process than simply heating the compound, vaporizing and condensing it, for in order to save all of the aromatic oils a process called *fractional distillation* must be used. Now different compounds have different boiling points and, consequently, they vaporize at different temperatures. The lightest oil passes over first and this is cooled and run off; then the temperature is raised and the next heavier oil is vaporized, cooled and run off, and this process is repeated until all the different oils, or *fractions*, as they are called, have been obtained. The compound which remains behind in the still is real camphor but it is still far from being as pure and white as camphor distilled from the camphor tree.

Brown sugar is just as sweet as white granulated sugar but no one wants to use brown sugar in his coffee if he can possibly get refined sugar even though the former is cheaper. The same preference holds good for camphor, and the public will not buy it if it is not just as white as the natural product. So the brown synthetic camphor must be refined; this is done by extracting every vestige of the oils that remain behind after distillation by forcing it through a filter press. Still the camphor is not perfectly white and to get rid of the remaining trace of color it is slowly evaporated and this drives out the water that contains the remaining impurities which color it. The final operation is to force a stream of air across the liquid camphor in the evaporating pan and this blows particles of it into a chamber where they are crystallized into snow-white flakes of pure camphor.

Making Synthetic Rubber.—The uses of rubber are so many that there never was a time when it was a drug on the market, and since the motorcar has become the common mode of transportation, the demand for it has increased by leaps and bounds. There are two ways by which more rubber can be had and these are (1) to plant more rubber trees, and (2) make it synthetically. Now caoutchouc, that is raw rubber, as it comes from the tree (see Chapter IV) has the formula of $C_{10}H_{16}$, which means that each rubber molecule is made up of 10 atoms of carbon and 16 atoms of hydrogen.

The nearest compound to rubber is a liquid called *isoprene* which has a chemical formula of C_5H_8; in other words it takes just half the number of carbon atoms and hydrogen atoms to make up a molecule of it as it takes to make up a molecule of rubber. Isoprene can be obtained from any one of a number of different gaseous, liquid and solid compounds, such as *acetylene, ethylene,* and *benzene*, all of which belong to the same family of hydrocarbons. It can also be made from *turpentine* and plants that contain *starch*.

Acetylene, which is made by the reaction of *calcium carbide* and *water*, has a formula of C_2H_2; *ethylene*, which is found in mineral, coal and water gas, has a formula of C_2H_4, while benzene, or *benzole* as it is sometimes called, is obtained from coal-tar when illuminating gas is made; it is a liquid and has a formula of C_6H_6. Turpentine, as you have just learned, is formed of $C_{10}H_{16}$, which is, curiously, exactly the same as the formula for rubber; it is obtained from pine trees, while starch, which is found in the roots of various plants, like the potato, the base of leaves, like the onion and certain seed, like corn, is built up of $C_6H_{10}O_5$. It is easy to see that all of these compounds have in them the necessary elements for making rubber, although the number of atoms of carbon usually falls short of the number that is contained in a molecule of rubber.

Since turpentine and rubber have exactly the same number of atoms of carbon and hydrogen atoms in the make-up of their molecules you may wonder why one is a liquid with a certain set of properties, and the other is a solid with another set of properties. The reason is that the carbon atoms are arranged in them differently, so that in order to make rubber you must not only have the same number of carbon atoms in each molecule of your synthetic compound as there are in the natural one but they must be held together in precisely the same fashion. This adds to the interest of the problem and the difficulty of successfully solving it.

A story has been going the rounds of the rubber world for the last thirty years to the effect that Prof. Tilden, a British chemist, had found, pieces of rubber in a bottle of *isoprene*, made from turpentine, which he had placed on a shelf. But try as he would the Professor was unable to again induce the isoprene to change into rubber, though he probably set a good many bottles of it on the shelf thereafter. So he has had to be content ever since to bask in the reflected glory of having been the first to observe the change.

In 1894, Dr. Matthews, of Manchester University, attacked the problem in a different way—the experimental way. He didn't wait for isoprene to change of its own accord into rubber but he finally found that it would change over by heating it with the *metal sodium*. As a cheap process for making metal sodium had been discovered by Castner in 1886 the cost of this element was of small consequence, but the trouble was that isoprene obtained from turpentine was too expensive a raw material to start with.

Since isoprene from turpentine was too costly to make synthetic rubber a commercial success, the next effort was to extract it (isoprene) from *starch*, and this in turn was obtained from the potato, which contains about twenty per cent of it. To get the isoprene from the starch it was fermented by means of *yeast* when it was converted into *fusel oil*, which is a kind of poisonous alcohol. By treating the fusel oil with chlorine, isoprene results.

Another way to make synthetic rubber is to use *acetone*, a liquid compound whose formula is C_3H_6O; this is made by heating *calcium acetate* and *lime*. Now when acetone and *acetylene gas* are chemically combined the resulting compound is isoprene. During the World War when the supply of rubber from Brazil and Africa was cut off from Germany, her chemists made synthetic rubber from acetone and acetylene gas in considerable quantities, but it was far from being up to the standard and it cost much more than the natural product in times of peace.

CHAPTER XV

THE MAGIC OF COAL-TAR

When coal gas first began to be manufactured for cooking and lighting purposes, the "gas house" was shunned by the surrounding neighborhood because of the vile-smelling refuse.

This pile of so-called refuse was composed chiefly of coal-tar, one of the by-products formed in the process of making illuminating gas, and as valuable as the chief product itself, for the black, smelly, sticky stuff contains the makings of brilliant dyes, beneficial drugs, exquisite perfumes and delicious flavors. But for many years it was thrown away.

What a Ton of Coal Contains.—When illuminating gas is made, *bituminous coal*, that is *soft coal* (see Chapter III) is placed in a retort and distilled. When heat is applied to the retort the coal is made successively to yield various solid, liquid, and gaseous compounds. The four chief products obtained from the destructive distillation of the coal, as it is called, are *illuminating gas*, *ammoniacal liquid* (see Chapter VIII), *coal-tar* and *coke*, and all of these compounds are now made use of so that nothing is allowed to go to waste. From a ton of soft coal there is made 12,000 cubic feet of gas, 2/3 of a ton of coke, 20 pounds of *ammonium sulphate* (which is made from the ammoniacal liquor) and 120 pounds of *tar*. Of these products only the latter interests us just now.

Stored-Up Sunshine.—In the black, sticky, ill-smelling coal-tar is stored up the sunshine and the rainbow tints of the tropical *carboniferous age*. From the coal-tar that is extracted from a ton of coal the following products, or *crudes* as they are called, are obtained by distilling it, and the figures after each one give, roughly, the amount contained in it. *Phenol*, that is *carbolic acid*, ½ pound; *benzene*, 15 pounds; *toluene*, 3 pounds; *xylene*, 1½ pounds; *naphthalene*, ⅜ pound; *anthracene*, ¼ pound, and *pitch*, 80 pounds. Now some of these compounds are liquids and some are solids but none of them has any color, though they do have distinctive odors. To make dyes or drugs of them they must be treated with other compounds.

To get the carbolic acid out of coal-tar it is treated with *sodium hydroxide*, that is *caustic soda*, which dissolves it out. By heating carbolic acid with nitric and sulphuric acids bright, yellow, needle-like crystals are formed and these are *picric acid*, or *trinitrophenol*, as the chemists call it. Picric acid (see Chapter VII) is extensively used in peace times as a yellow dye for silk and wool and it was in great demand during the War as an explosive.

Benzene and Aniline.—Benzene, or *benzole*, as it was formerly called, is one of the lighter oils that comes from coal-tar. Benzene dissolves raw rubber and when acted on by dilute *sulphur chloride* the rubber hardens in very much the same way as when it is heated, that is *vulcanized* (see Chapter IX). This process is called *cold vulcanizing*, or *cold curing*, which is a better name. But benzene has a far more important use than that of curing rubber, and this is to convert it into *nitro-benzene*. To make this compound the benzene is treated with nitric acid when a heavy, oily liquid results which has an odor very much like that of bitter almonds. It is from nitro-benzene that *aniline* is produced and from this compound, which is a colorless oil, *aniline dyes* of many colors are made.

Aniline is one of the seven wonders of chemical discovery, as you will shortly see. To make it from nitro-benzene, iron borings from a lathe, and *hydrochloric (muriatic) acid* are put together with the nitro-benzene into a chamber, and the steam is turned on. By the action of the hydrochloric acid on the iron, hydrogen is set free by the former and this combines with the nitro-benzene, when aniline and water are formed. These are then separated by distilling them, when the aniline is ready to be used for making dyes and other products.

How Coal-Tar Dyes Were Discovered.—Away back in the middle of the last century a boy of eighteen named William Perkin who was an ardent amateur chemist got a great idea. The sole supply of *quinine* was then and is yet made of *Peruvian bark;* as it was very scarce at that time, and therefore costly, young Perkin conceived that it was possible to make the drug by mixing together certain other compounds—that is to produce it synthetically. If he could do so, a fortune was ready and waiting for him so he began working with this end in view. In one of his experiments he treated aniline with *potassium dichromate*, a red salt formed of the *metal potassium*, the *metal chromium*[22] and oxygen, but instead of getting quinine he got a muddy precipitate, which not more than one chemist in a thousand would have thought it worth while to investigate.

But William Perkin was the thousandth man. He looked at it long and curiously and then poured a little alcohol on it when lo! he found he had made a gorgeous purple dye and to which he gave the name of *mauve*. He called it *mauve* from the French flower of that name, but which we know as the *mallow*. This then was the first coal-tar dye and for a long time it was widely used for dyeing silk and wool, but owing to its tendency to fade in the sunlight it has been displaced by other and faster dyes.

The Discovery of Magenta.—The success of the new dye spread like wildfire, and other chemists everywhere tried to duplicate it by using other agents than *potassium dichromate* to oxidize the aniline oil. First Renard and Faure of France used *arsenic*, a brittle, steel gray element whose properties are very much like *phosphorus*, with the aniline, but instead of getting mauve they obtained that wonderful crimson dye known as *magenta*. The dye itself, however, does not contain any arsenic but is a salt formed when *rosaniline* combines with an acid. Not

---

[22] It gets its name from the Greek word *chroma* which means surface color.

only is magenta used directly for dyeing but, like aniline, it forms the starting point for making many other dyes. One of the dyes made from it in the early days was called *phosphine* which gave a beautiful orange color. It is not called by that name now, as *phosphine* in the chemistry of to-day is a *gaseous phosphoretted hydrogen*. Another early aniline dye was *Nicholson's blue*, but instead of producing the color direct, the goods were first dipped into the dye, which was colorless, and then dipped into a solution of weak sulphuric acid when the blue color was brought out. This was termed an *adjective* dye.

Dyes and Explosives from Toluene.—*Toluene*, or *toluol* as it is often called, is a colorless, inflammable liquid that is very much like benzene; when it is treated in the same way, that is with nitric acid, it is changed into *nitrotoluene* and from this aniline is likewise produced. Although only ⅜ of a pound of naphthalene can be had from a ton of coal and 3 pounds of toluene can be had from the same amount, a process for making *indigo* from the last named compound was discarded in favor of the first because it was in great demand for making *trinitrotoluene*, that is the explosive commonly called *TNT*. So we get our synthetic indigo not from toluene but from naphthalene. The difference between nitrotoluene and trinitrotoluene is that the toluene of the first has only *one* group of nitrogen and oxygen atoms combined with it, while the second has *three* groups of nitrogen and oxygen atoms. When three groups of nitrogen atoms are combined with the toluene the compound becomes very unstable and this accounts for its explosiveness.

Alizarin from Anthracene.—For many years prior to 1869 a plant called *madder* was cultivated on a large scale in India, Turkey, Persia and some parts of Southern Europe. Its value lay in its roots which contained a coloring compound that was used as a dye to produce the far-famed *Turkey red*. As early as 1828 Robiquet and Colin, of France, isolated the active principle of the madder root that actually produced the red color; this they called *Alizarin*, from *alazari*, which is the Arabic name for *Turkey red*, but what the crystals were made of they did not know.

Then four years later Dumas and Laurent succeeded in extracting a new compound from coal-tar and to this the name of *anthracene* was given. The next gap, and it was a big one, was bridged shortly before 1869 by Graebe and Liebermann, of Germany, who distilled some *alizarin*, made from madder, with *zinc dust* and obtained *anthracene*. This was the key that unlocked an entirely new series of dyes, for since anthracene could be had from alizarin it ought to be possible to reverse the direction of the reaction and convert anthracene into alizarin; and this the chemists did without any great trouble. It was the first time in history that a dye made by nature had been duplicated synthetically by man.

The commercial world went wild over the achievement but, like many other synthetic products which have since been brought out, alizarin made from anthracene cost more than when it was extracted from the madder plant. But it was not long before both the British and German chemists had improved the process for making synthetic alizarin, and anthracene, which had previously been sold for axle-grease, went up in price to several hundred dollars a ton, while the business of growing madder fast declined and then went under altogether.

Alizarin is known as an *adjective dye* because the goods to be dyed must be dipped first in a solution made of the oxide of some metal, as iron, aluminum or chromium; then when it is dipped into the dye a precipitate is formed in the goods that cannot be washed out. A dye, such as *indigo*, which dyes the goods on coming in contact with it, is called a *substantive dye*.

Naphthalene and Indigo.—The first crude product to be obtained from coal-tar was *naphthalene*. It was discovered by Gordon, of England, in 1819 and as it consisted of white crystals made up of pearly scales, it was looked upon with wonder for some time, for it was not easy in those days to see how so beautiful a substance could come from such a black, sticky mass. Naphthalene was first obtained from the heavy oils of coal-tar which contain considerable amounts of it, and next it was produced by passing benzene through red-hot tubes.

It is now made from *light oil* and *creosote oil;* the latter is the residue that is left behind after anthracene is separated from the crude oil. To obtain naphthalene from these oils, *caustic soda* is thoroughly mixed with them and this dissolves out the phenol (carbolic acid) and the *cresol* (cresylic acid) that is in them. The mixture then separates into water, with the acids in it, at the bottom of the vat and the oil, which contains the naphthalene, on top.

Naphthalene has largely taken the place of the more costly camphor as an insecticide, and this is the compound that *moth-balls* are made of. It is also much used for preserving insects, moths and butterflies for collections. But its chief use is in making dyes and many tons of it are used for this purpose every year. Nor are naphthalene dyes by any means limited to a single color but range from the most delicate yellows to the brightest reds and greens.

If you have ever seen clothes washed at home you will remember that the laundress puts *bluing* into the *rinse-water*, which is the last water they are put through, to make them white. The bluing is *indigo*, a dye-stuff that is as old as civilization itself, at any rate the Egyptians used it before the pyramids were built. For centuries all the indigo that was used came from a bushy plant which was originally found in the East Indies, and so it was called *indigo*.

The coloring matter was extracted from the plants by putting them in vats of water and letting them ferment. To make a dye-stuff of it the indigo was treated with sulphuric acid, when it absorbed the hydrogen, and a soluble and colorless compound resulted which was called *white indigo*. After goods are dyed with it they are exposed to the air which fixes the insoluble blue indigo in them for all time.

About 1840, Fritzsche, a German chemist, found, when he was experimenting with *indigo*, that by distilling it with *caustic potash* the vapor, which passed over, on being cooled formed colorless crystals. He was not long in finding out that the crystallized compound he had made was identical with indigo and so he called it *analin*, from the Arabic word *anil* which means blue. Later on, aniline was produced from coal-tar, but no one knew how to extract indigo from it until 1879 when Adolph von Bayer discovered a way to do it; but indigo produced by his process was more costly than that obtained from the plant.

After experimenting for many years he found he could make it from three of the different *crudes* of coal-tar, the cheapest one being from naphthalene, and yet his process could not compete with nature. Then in 1894 the Badische Anilin und Soda Fabrik, of Germany, took it up and after spending several million dollars and fifteen years in research work its chemists evolved a commercial process for making *synthetic indigo;* and the indigo it made was not only better than natural indigo but it was so much cheaper that the indigo growers had to go the way of the madder growers—that is out of business.

The starting point for making indigo is, then, naphthalene but as the process is complicated and the reactions numerous we shall only give you an outline of it. First the naphthalene is changed into *phthalic* (pronounced *thal-ic*) *acid* by heating it with *sulphuric acid* and a little *mercury*. The *phthalic* acid is then heated to drive off the water in it when it becomes *phthalic anhydride*. (An anhydride is a compound which when dissolved in water forms an acid.) The anhydride is next changed into *phthalimide* by heating it with ammonia and this, in turn, is converted into *anthranilic acid* by treating it with *caustic soda* and *chlorine*.

Now by means of *monochloracetic acid* the anthranilic acid is changed into *phenyl-glycine ortho-carboxylic acid*, which is called *phenyl-glycine acid* for short. This latter compound is melted with *caustic potash* which then gives *indoxyl*, and this is getting pretty close to indigo. A stream of air is now forced through the mass which oxidizes it and changes it into *indigotine;* which is *indigo blue*. To make a dye-stuff of it, the indigo is treated with sulphuric acid, when *white indigo*, or *indigo white* as it is called, is produced.

Making Drugs from Coal-Tar.—Not only are beautiful colors obtained from coal-tar but wonderful drugs as well. You will remember that William Perkin was at work trying to make *quinine* from aniline when he discovered he had produced *mauve* instead. Now while chemists have never been able to make quinine from coal-tar the work they did along this line has resulted in some new and even more valuable drugs. There is a compound extracted from coal-tar called *quinoline* and it is from this that chemists have long tried to obtain *quinine*. Instead, they discovered among others a drug known as *thallin* which was once used as a remedy for yellow fever, but the after-effect of the drug on the patient was nearly as bad as the disease and its use was, for this reason, given up. The first coal-tar drug to find a permanent place on the druggists' shelf was *antipyrin*. This drug was made by Dr. Knorr, of Germany, in 1883, from aniline and it has been largely used ever since instead of quinine as a cold and fever remedy and for relieving headaches.

Then *acetanilide*, or *antifebrine* as it is sometimes called, was discovered in the same works where the manufacture of antipyrin was carried on. It is extracted from aniline by treating the latter with *acetic acid*. It is also used as a remedy for fever and is especially useful in neuralgia. Carbolic acid, as you read earlier in this chapter, is one of the *crudes* that is obtained by distilling coal-tar. *Salicylic acid* was formerly obtained from the bark of the willow tree, but Kobe made it from carbolic acid in 1874 so that it is to-day a synthetic product. About 1904 Adolph von Bayer produced a new drug which he called *aspirin;* it has a wide and ever growing use as a headache remedy and it is especially good in neuritis and rheumatism. Its curative property is due to the salicylic acid in it. *Aspirin* is simply a trade name given it, for it is really *acetyl salicylic acid* and is formed by the action of *acetic acid* on *salicylic acid.*

Phenacetin is another acetyl compound made from carbolic acid. It is older than aspirin and is a quicker and more certain remedy for headache than the latter, but it also has a greater effect on the heart and should, therefore, only be used by persons who have no heart trouble. Among other coal-tar drugs are *soporifics* such as *veronal, medinal,* and *sulphonal,* and *anæsthetics* like *eucain, cocain,* and *novocain.*

Veronal, which is also called *barbitone,* is a sleep producing drug and it will insure a good night's sleep no matter how troubled the mind may be. It is derived from *barbituric acid*, or *malonyl-urea* as the chemists call it, and is produced from coal-tar. *Medinal* is also a sleep inducer and is likewise derived from barbituric acid. But the greatest of all these soporifics is *sulphonal* which is used both as a hypnotic and as an anæsthetic. It will not only induce a profound sleep but a refreshing one as well. It is a heavy crystalline compound and is made by oxidizing *ethyl mercaptan* and acetone.

Cocain, as its name indicates, was first obtained from the *coca-tree* and was largely used in the painless extraction of teeth. Then eucain followed and now novocain is in favor with the dentists. All of these local anæsthetics are made purer and better from coal-tar than when extracted from plants.

Besides the above drugs there are many others produced either directly or indirectly from coal-tar and other compounds. The chemists have acquired, what is called in physics, *momentum*, and, having got a good start,

nothing can stop them in their efforts to duplicate nature's drugs and to make new ones.

CHAPTER XVI

MAKING PERFUMES AND FLAVORS

SCENTS, that is fragrant scents, and flavors are so closely related that they are usually considered together, but here we shall treat them separately and tell you how they are obtained from nature as well as how they are made by chemical synthesis. In the first place, you may or may not know that the words *smell* and *odor* do not mean the same thing.

Your nose is the *organ of smell* and it contains the *olfactory nerves* which lead to your brain. In order for these nerves to excite the sensation of smell in the brain-cells the odorous substance, or compound, must be capable of giving off minute particles, that is molecules of it, and these must come into direct contact with them. Gaseous compounds do this the most readily—in fact too readily. Liquids vaporize easily and perfumes are, for this reason, chiefly formed of them, while some solids give off their molecules but to a very much lesser extent. Now while it is usually easy to describe what the eyes see, the ears hear and the hands feel, it is a very different matter to describe what the nose smells; we can only say that the odor is good or bad, or sweet or acrid, but to tell its characteristics is next to impossible. But since perfumes are formed of known elements in definite combinations, efforts have been made to classify them, but nothing very definite has as yet resulted from the experiments.

What Essential Oils Are.—Oils are divided into two general classes known as the *fixed oils* and the *volatile oils*. There are several differences between them and among these it may be said that fixed oils *do not* evaporate and volatile oils *do* evaporate at room temperature. You can always tell to which class an oil belongs by putting a drop of it on paper; if it leaves a lasting stain it is a fixed oil but if it evaporates and leaves no stain it is a volatile oil. Another way to tell is by twisting the cork in the neck of the bottle that contains it; if it turns without making a sound it is a fixed oil, but if it squeaks it is a volatile oil. When you heat the fixed oils to more than 500 degrees Fahrenheit, they give off bad and suffocating odors and when greater heat is applied they break up into their constituent parts; on heating volatile oils they vaporize but do not give off rank odors or decompose.

The fixed oils will make soap while volatile oils will not. To make a little soap all you need to do is to put some fixed oil into a test-tube and add some *caustic potash* to it. Now heat it over the flame of an alcohol lamp or a Bunsen burner, when the *alkali*, as the potash is called, will combine with the oil and *soft soap* will be formed. Finally the fixed oils cannot be dissolved in *ether* or *alcohol*, while the volatile oils dissolve easily in either of them.

Essential oils, of which perfumes and flavoring extracts are made, are volatile oils, and before the days of coal-tar chemistry they were obtained from plants; for instance, the essential oil of violet was produced from fresh violets, the essential oil of roses, or *attar of roses* as it is called, was made from fresh roses. In some plants the oil is contained in the seed, in others in the leaves and still in others in the roots. It is these essential oils or the active principles in them, that give various kinds of flowers their sweet odors.

Some Coal-Tar Perfumes.—Now some, if not all, of the essential oils can be made from coal-tar crudes, and those obtained by the chemist are just as sweet and delicate as those produced by nature. The processes by which chemists make them are identical with those by which he manufactures synthetic dyes, and aniline furnishes the raw material for the starting point of many of them.

Scent of New Mown Hay.—Some plants have in them an essential oil called *coumarin* whose odor is like that of new mown hay. Among these are the bean of the *Tonka, Tonqua,* or *Tonquin,* as it is variously spelled, the leaves of the *woodruff,* a common plant of Europe, and *sweet clover*. The way to make coumarin from coal-tar was discovered by William Perkin, that prince of experimentalists, in 1868.

He started with *salicylic aldehyde; salicylic acid* is made of *carbolic acid*, and an *aldehyde* is a substance that is neither an alcohol nor an acid but stands just between them. Carbolic acid is one of the crudes of coal-tar but it can also be made from *acetylene*. This being true, coumarin becomes a strictly synthetic product, for a start can be made with the elements of *carbon* and *hydrogen* and these combined to form *acetylene*; this is changed into *benzene*; the latter is converted into *carbolic acid* and from this *salicylic aldehyde* is obtained which is finally made into *coumarin*. Here then is a clear-cut case where the chemist can start with two elements, one a solid and the other a gas, and build them up adding various other atoms to them until he has a crystalline compound like that obtained from the plants and which has precisely the same odor.

Scent of the Lilac and Lily of the Valley.—Another synthetic product is a solid compound called *terpineol*, which is a kind of alcohol. There are two kinds of it and these have odors exactly like the lilac and lily of the valley, hence they are largely used in making perfumes that go by these attractive names. In making terpineol, *turpentine oil* is taken as the starting point and on adding to this a solution of *alcohol* and *nitric acid* there crystallizes out of it a compound called *terpin hydrate*. By hydrate is meant a compound that is formed by the union of molecules of water with the molecules of some other compound in which the arrangement of the atoms is not disturbed. Next water and a small quantity of sulphuric acid are added to the terpin hydrate when the solution is distilled; this gets rid of the water and the thick liquid left behind is terpineol; when this is cooled it crystallizes and is ready to be made into lilac or lily of the valley perfume.

Scent of Attar of Roses.—This fragrant essential oil is obtained from the petals of roses; it was originally a product of Persia, which accounts for its name, for *atar* in the Persian language means *breath perfume*, or its equivalent. Later it was made in different oriental countries, especially in Arabia and in India. It is also called *otto of roses* perhaps for the reason that when the Germans began to make it synthetically they thought it fitting to Germanize the name. Attar of roses made from fresh flowers is enormously expensive for it takes a hundred pounds of rose petals to make one-fourth of an ounce of it.

Although the essential oil of the rose is made up of nearly two dozen different compounds, *geraniol* is the chief one. It is a colorless, odorless essence and is the one that gives *geranium oil* and *rose oil* their pleasing and distinctive scents. When geraniol is oxidized it gives *citral* from which *ionone* is formed, and ionone, in turn, is the synthetic essence of which practically all violet waters and violet perfumes are made. To *oxidize* a compound means that it is made to combine chemically with oxygen.

It was in one of the great laboratories of Germany that the essential oil of the rose was first analyzed, that is each one of its active principles, or essences, was isolated; and this having been done the chemists proceeded to reverse the process and synthetize the essential oil, that is to build it up out of its various elements and compounds. And so excellent is the product that the expert olfactory organs of the perfumer cannot tell the one that man has made from the one that nature has made. The only difference is that the first costs in the neighborhood of five dollars a pound and the second costs something like five hundred dollars a pound.

Scent of the Violet.—The essential oil of fresh violets is about as scarce as *radium* but violet toilet waters and violet perfumes are the most plentiful scents on the market. How is it? The secret is not hard to discover for the essential oil is now made in laboratories by the ton, and so when you pay two dollars for a small bottle of toilet water, or five or six dollars for a still smaller bottle of violet perfume you don't need to feel that the perfumer is cheating himself.

Thirty years ago two German chemists, Tiemann and Krüger, began to analyze the essential oil of the violet to find out exactly what it was made of. The first difficulty they encountered was that they could not get enough of the oil to experiment with. Now there is a plant with sword-like leaves that is called the *iris*, or *fleur-de-lis* and whose root is known as *orris-root*. The root of the East Indian species when dried has about the same odor as that of the violet and, hence, the essential oil in it must be the same as that of the former. When they had isolated the active principle they called it *irone* and it was found that each molecule of it was made up of 13 atoms of carbon, 20 atoms of hydrogen and 1 atom of oxygen, or $C_{13}H_{20}O$.

While working on the synthetic production of irone another compound was discovered whose odor

MAKING PERFUMES AND FLAVORS

was identical with that of fresh violets and to this they gave the name of *ionone*. This compound is made by heating *citral* and *acetone* together with *caustic soda* when *pseudo-ionone* is formed. (*Pseudo* means *false* and, hence, the name means literally *false-ionone*.) However false it may be, when it is boiled with sulphuric acid it breaks up into two compounds both of which are ionone but each of which is a shade different from the other. The first is known as α *ionone*, that is *alpha* ionone, and the second as β *ionone*, or *beta* ionone. These two ionones are as alike as two peas, even the arrangement of the atoms of their molecules being the same, but there is one atom more of hydrogen in the β ionone than there is in the α ionone. To the ordinary person the odors of these ionones smell exactly alike but a perfumer can detect a slight difference.

The α ionone is exceedingly sweet and its odor is precisely that of the essential oil of fresh violets while the β ionone is a shade less sweet and refined and this is used for scenting toilet soaps. Again when the two ionones are mixed together they are sold as the *oil of orris-root*.

Scents of Other Flowers.—The odors of many other flowers are also produced synthetically. Thus the odor of the *heliotrope* is duplicated by a compound called *piperonal*; this is a white, crystalline compound that is formed by oxidizing *piperic acid* (which is obtained from the *pepper plant*) with *potassium permanganate*. Piperonal is very closely allied to *vanillin*, a flavoring extract which will be described shortly. *Neroli* is another interesting essential oil used in making perfumes. It is found in various flowers such as the *jasmine*, the *tube-rose*, and *ylang-ylang*, and is also obtained by distilling *bitter orange*. It is made synthetically by treating *anthranilic acid* with *methyl alcohol* and *hydrogen chloride*.

Some Coal-Tar Flavors.—We usually take the word *flavor* to mean a peculiar and pleasing quality of food that affects the sense of taste. As a matter of exact statement the flavor of food not only affects the sense of taste but in a large measure the sense of smell as well. To be able to sense the flavor of food it must be soluble, that is capable of being dissolved by the gastric juice of the mouth and it must then be brought into direct contact with the tongue and other parts of the mouth.

The *taste organs*, or *end-organs* as they are called, which receive the stimulus of taste are formed of *taste-buds*, or *gustatory buds*, that are located principally on the upper surface and the edges of the tongue; there are also some taste buds on the soft palate and the larynx. These sensory nerve buds are connected with the brain by three sets of cranial nerves, since many of the sensations of flavor that you get are really caused by the odors that are given off by the food after it is dissolved in your mouth and carried up to the olfactory nerves.

There are only four fundamental, that is distinct tastes, and these are sweet and bitter, and sour and saline. The sweet and bitter tastes are set up by the chemical action of the food as it dissolves, while the sour taste is the perception of acids, and the saline taste is the perception of salts and alkalis. The taste buds at the tip of the tongue are most responsive to sweet flavors, those on the edges of the tongue respond best to sour flavors, those on top of the tongue to salt, and those at the back of the tongue to bitter substances.

The Flavor of Vanilla.—Soon after Perkin discovered how to make coumarin from coal-tar in 1868, Tiemann made *vanillin* which is the essential oil of the vanilla pod. Now while vanillin can be built up of free carbon, hydrogen, and oxygen and it can also be obtained from coal-tar, it takes a number of processes to do so which make its production by these means too costly. So it is produced by more simple means, that is the start is made with *eugenol,* which is the essence of the *oil of cloves,* and by oxidizing the latter vanillin results. The fact that the starting compound is obtained from a plant instead of coal-tar does not make it any the less a synthetic product, for no matter whether the start is made with the original free elements, from coal-tar or from plants, the resultant vanillin is in all respects identical with that which is extracted from the vanilla pod.

The Flavor of Wintergreen.—It takes a long stretch of the imagination to link up the essence of wintergreen with that of carbolic acid but the former is nevertheless now made from the latter. In other words, wintergreen is a coal-tar flavor. To make *oil of wintergreen,* carbolic acid is treated with carbon dioxide which converts it into salicylic acid. Methyl alcohol, that is wood alcohol, and sulphuric acid are next added to the salicylic acid and the mixture is heated, when *methyl salicylate* is produced and this is oil of wintergreen which is exactly the same as that obtained from wintergreen berries.

Other Synthetic Flavors.—Besides the flavors described above, there are many others made by the action of various kinds of acids on different alcohols. These combinations yield *ethyl butyrate* which is the flavor of pineapple; *amyl-acetate* which is the flavor of the pear; while compounds of ether produce the flavors of strawberry and other berries. As a matter of fact, there is not a flavor of any known plant which cannot be reproduced in the laboratory and many of them are made and sold in large quantities.

CHAPTER XVII

ELECTRIC FURNACE PRODUCTS

JUST as the electric arc is the brightest light that man has yet produced so, also, does it develop the greatest heat that is known. When water boils, its temperature is 212 degrees Fahrenheit; the heat of an ordinary coal fire is about 600 degrees which is just a little more than is needed to melt aluminum; as iron melts at 2,912 degrees, a hotter fire than the usual ones is needed and this can be obtained by supplying more oxygen to the fuel either by means of a bellows, or by a centrifugal blower.

The Heat of an Electric Arc.—By passing a current of electricity between the points of a pair of carbon rods, called *electrodes*, which are slightly separated, a temperature of 7,000 degrees is reached and this is twice as high as is needed to melt platinum. But this is not nearly the limit of the heat that can be obtained from the electric arc, for if you enclose it in an airtight vessel and pump air into it until the pressure is 300 pounds to the square inch, instead of 15 pounds which is the ordinary pressure of air, a temperature of

14,000 degrees results and this outdoes the heat of the sun of equal area.

You have seen in the chapter on *Fire, Heat, and Fuel* some of the wonders that can be performed with the ordinary temperatures that primitive man had at his command; but as the heat becomes greater more and more wonders can be worked with it, in that compounds can be broken up into their respective substances and elements, which have never been broken up before; but what is of far more worth, elements and substances can be combined so that new compounds are formed the like of which Nature never made in her laboratories and mankind never knew before.

Sir Humphry Davy, a British scientist, produced the first electric arc light in 1800, and this he did by connecting two pieces of charcoal with an electric battery; on holding the pieces of charcoal in contact with each other and then separating them slightly a dazzling light arched itself between them. The first *electric furnace* was a more elaborate apparatus though the principle was exactly the same as the arc lamp. Dr. Robert Hare, a chemist of the University of Pennsylvania, is credited not only with having made it, which he did early in the nineteenth century, but he is also credited with having "changed charcoal into graphite, separated phosphorus and obtained the metal calcium from their respective compounds," as well as to have made calcium carbide.

How Calcium Carbide is Made.—In the chapter on *How Plants Live and Grow* we explained how acetylene gas, which was once used for motor-car lighting and is now largely used in *oxyacetylene welding* is made. In making acetylene gas the calcium carbide is disintegrated, that is broken down by the action of the water which falls drop by drop upon it; and now let us find out how calcium carbide is made.

Calcium is a metal and it is the fifth most plentiful element that goes to make up the earth's crust; it is little known, however, as it is always found combined with other substances, generally in limestone, marble, gypsum and chalk and it gets its name from *calx* which is the Latin word for white and means *lime*. It is a white metal like aluminum but so soft it can be kneaded with the fingers. Metallic calcium is obtained by fusing *calcium chloride* in a graphite crucible and passing an electric current through it, so that it is itself an electric furnace product, though an element.

Calcium carbide is made by heating coke and *quicklime*, that is *calcium oxide* in an electric furnace when the heat of the electric arc makes the carbon of the coke and the calcium in the quicklime combine, when *calcium carbide* and *carbon monoxide* are formed. The carbon monoxide is a gas and this is allowed to pass off into the air. The calcium carbide is a mass of crystals and these, when pure, are colorless; more often the carbide is only of fair quality, when they are a reddish color, and when of poor quality they have a grayish color.

Making calcium carbide in the electric furnace remained a laboratory experiment until the *dynamo*, as a direct current electric machine is called, was invented. The manufacture of calcium carbide on a commercial scale, however, did not begin until electricity was generated cheaply by the great hydro-electric plant at Niagara Falls. The process of making calcium carbide on a commercial scale consists of breaking up the coke and lime into pieces about as large as stove coal and dumping them into an electric furnace. This is formed of a sheet-iron box, some six feet high with flanged wheels so that it can run on a track. The electrodes are made of graphite and are mounted so that they can be set into the furnace in an upright position. When the heat produced by the arc reaches 3,500 degrees Centigrade the carbon and calcium combine and form a liquid mass; the electrodes are now lifted out of the box

HEROULT ELECTRIC FURNACE

A high-temperature furnace of 500 pounds capacity in use by the Bureau of Standards.

and the latter is rolled away and another box charged with coke and lime is run into its place. In this way the same electrodes can be used continuously and no time is lost waiting for the calcium carbide to cool.

How Carborundum is Made.—If, now, instead of calcium there is used *silica* in the form of crushed quartz or sand, and this is mixed with coke and they are brought to a high enough temperature in an electric furnace, they will combine and form *silicon carbide*, which is a compound of *silicon* and *carbon*. This substance which is made up of crystals is harder than emery and nearly as hard as the diamond. It makes, therefore, a fine abrasive and has all but supplanted the ordinary whetstone and emery grinding wheel.

Now silicon carbide is best known in the United States by the trade name of *carborundum*, and in Canada it is called *carbolon*. While Hare was the first one to make carborundum he neither knew what he had made nor did he give it a name. Indeed, it was not until 1885 that the Cowles Brothers made carborundum in a furnace heated by an electric arc whose source of current was the dynamo, but even they did not know the exact nature of the compound they had produced.

The next man to tackle the problem was E. A. Acheson and the first silicon carbide that he made was on quite a small scale. He placed a pair of graphite electrodes in a pot and packed sand and charcoal around them; then he connected the electrodes with a dynamo and switched on the current. After twenty-four hours or so he switched off the current, took out the electrodes and found that they were covered with black, steel-blue and deep yellow crystals the like of which Nature had never made and which reflected the light like gems of the first water. He sold these crystals for nearly fifty cents an ounce and found a market for all he could make. Soon he began to produce silicon carbide, which he named *carborundum*, in large lots using the cheap electricity generated by the Falls of Niagara, and so was able to market it for a few cents a pound.

The furnaces used for the production of carborundum are laid up of brick without mortar and are about five feet high, six feet wide and sixteen feet long. The electrodes are huge carbon rods which set in the furnace lengthwise and in between them is packed a core of coke which heats the charge around it by conduction. Around this is placed the charge which

CARBORUNDUM CRYSTAL
Manufactured in the electric furnaces at Niagara Falls.

ELECTRIC FURNACE PRODUCTS

consists of sand, coke, sawdust and a very little salt. The purpose of the sawdust is to make the charge porous so that the carbon monoxide can escape easily, while the salt is added to make the charge fuse more readily. The current is now switched on and this heats the charge to 3,500 degrees Centigrade when the *silicon* of the sand combines with the carbon of the coke and makes silicon carbide and carbon monoxide.

Other Silicon Products.—Besides carborundum there are several other electric furnace products that are made by fusing sand with other substances. One of these is *siloxicon* which is obtained by mixing sand with twice its weight of coal. Since it is not affected by high temperatures it is used for lining furnaces. Another form of carborundum is made by passing silicon vapor through carbon shapes when the latter is converted into *silundum*. This compound is largely used for electric resistances which have to be heated to high temperatures.

Then there are the *silicides*—compounds that have a bluish-white tint and which look like metal. To make one of them, sand and carbon and an oxide of an alkaline earth metal are mixed together and fused in an electric furnace. Still another electric furnace substance is *alundum* which is an artificial emery. It is made by fusing *bauxite*, an ore that contains about sixty per cent of *aluminum oxide*, and carbon at a high temperature. As the mass cools, crystals are formed, and these are crushed and roasted to remove any particles of metal that may remain in them, after which they are made into grinding wheels.

How Graphite is Made.—Carbon is one of the most plentiful elements that go to make up the earth's crust, and it is not only found in rocks of various kinds but one-half of all plant matter is formed of it. While carbon is an element all carbon is not alike; there are three distinct forms, the *diamond*, *graphite*, and what is called *amorphous carbon* which means that it is not crystallized. The diamond is pure carbon that has been crystallized by heat and pressure, and it is the hardest substance known. Graphite, or *black-lead*, as it is sometimes called, because it will mark on paper like lead and is used in making lead-pencils, is also a crystallized form of carbon, but it is entirely different from the diamond in that it is very soft and flaky. Because it is so soft and smooth it is used for lubricating machinery where in some cases it is better than oil. It was M. Moissan, a French chemist, who found that amorphous carbon could be changed into either diamond or graphite. The process he employed to make diamonds in the electric furnace will be found in the chapter on *Making Precious Stones*.

When carborundum is made in the electric furnace, graphite is formed around the core between the electrodes which is the hottest part of the charge, and this led to the making of graphite in large quantities. Before this method of producing graphite was discovered nearly all of it was obtained from deposits at Ticonderoga, N. Y., Brandon, Vt., and Sturbridge, Mass., but the electric furnace product is superior to that which nature made, and further there is no limit to the amount of it.

The way that graphite is produced is about like this, although chemists have not yet learned exactly what the reaction is: The silicon carbide is broken down by the high temperature, the silicon of it being set free as a vapor and the carbon deposited as graphite. The electric furnace in which graphite is made at Niagara Falls is about two feet high and wide and thirty feet long and through each end there is fixed a number of electrodes. Into this furnace is placed a charge consisting of sand and *anthracite coal* (hard coal) ground up together. Since coal will not conduct a current of electricity a carbon rod of small diameter is connected between the main electrodes in the ends of the furnace, and when the current is switched on it gets hot because it offers resistance to the passage of the current; in turn it heats the coal, making it a conductor.

The current is allowed to pass through the charge for twenty hours and the temperature during the run is in the neighborhood of 3,500 degrees Centigrade. Graphite electrodes which are used in electric arc furnaces are made in the same way as the loose graphite described above, only the charge is made up of petroleum, coke and sand and these substances are molded into rods of various sizes. The rods are then baked, when they are laid in the furnace where the current converts them into graphite electrodes.

How Phosphorus is Made.—Phosphorus in the form of *calcium phosphate*, commonly called *phosphate of lime*, is found in the bones of all animals in considerable quantities. While the element is a deadly poison, many of its compounds are most beneficial. In times past it was obtained by heating bones until they were white hot when the animal matter was burned out of them. To get the calcium out of them they are treated with sulphuric acid, when they are again heated to a high temperature, this time with carbon, when the pure phosphorus vaporizes and is caught and solidified under water.

Phosphorus is now made in the electric furnace either from bone-ash or mineral phosphate. Whichever material is used, the phosphate is mixed with sand and charcoal and then put into an electric furnace; the high temperature set up by the arc converts the charge into *phosphorus vapor*, *carbon monoxide*, and *slag*. The first is collected and condensed into a solid, the second, since it is a gas, passes off, and the last runs off in a melted stream.

How Carbon Disulphide is Made.—This compound is a volatile, colorless liquid which has a very bad odor and burns like gasoline. About the only use for it fifty years ago was to fill hollow glass prisms employed in experiments with the spectrum of the sun. Advances have been made since then and it is now largely used to kill insects and rodents, as a solvent for rubber and sulphur, and in making *artificial silk*.

Edward R. Taylor, an American chemist, was the first to make carbon disulphide in the electric furnace. The furnace he designed for producing it is different from those previously described in that it consists of a chimney-like apparatus about sixteen feet in diameter and forty feet in height. The charge is composed of charcoal and sulphur and the furnace is filled with the first, which is pulverized, while the sulphur is fed in at the top. A pair of horizontal electrodes are fitted into the furnace near the bottom and when the current is switched on, the heat of the arc burns the charcoal (carbon) and melts the sulphur, when the carbon and sulphur combine and produce *carbon disulphide* and *sulphur vapor*. The disulphide vapor ascends through the charge of charcoal and passes through a pipe near the top to the condensing chambers where it is cooled and becomes a liquid.

Making Alkali in the Electric Furnace.—This is a very recent process of making *chlorine* and *caustic soda* in large quantities. Chlorine you will remember is one of the good gases, when it is not used for war operations, while caustic soda, whose chemical name is *sodium hydroxide*, is largely used in making *soap* from fats, for bleaching, preparing paper pulp, and other purposes. In making chlorine and caustic soda in the electrolytic cell *sodium chloride*, which is our old friend common salt, is heated until it is decomposed.

In this is placed a carbon electrode, called the anode, to which the wire carrying the positive electricity from the dynamo is connected; the other electrode, called the *cathode*, to which the wire carrying the negative current from the dynamo is connected, is formed of melted lead. The cell is made gas-tight and over the anode there is an outlet for the chlorine to pass out into a containing chamber. When the current is switched on it decomposes the sodium chloride and the chlorine passes off, while the *sodium*, which is a metal, mixes with the melted lead and forms an alloy.

The melted alloy is then made to flow into another part of the cell where it is subjected to a blast of steam and this reacts on the sodium and forms a solution of caustic soda and hydrogen. The caustic soda, which is lighter than the melted lead, is drawn off through a valve, when the lead is again returned to the chamber where it becomes the cathode as before, while the hydrogen which has been set at liberty passes out through an outlet.

The Making of Metallic Sodium.—Two different electric furnace processes have been devised for producing the *metal sodium* on a large scale and, hence, making it cheaply. The first of these is the *Castner process*, so-called because it was gotten up by H. N. Castner, of Brooklyn, N. Y. In this process the caustic soda in a fused state is decomposed by the action of the electric current, when the metallic sodium floats upward through the melted solution. In the *Ashcroft process* the furnace consists of two separate tanks connected by a pipe. The melted sodium chloride (common salt) is decomposed by means of a lead cathode, when it forms an alloy with it as when alkalies are made. The melted alloy then flows through the pipe into the second tank where it comes into contact with the melted caustic soda. Again it is decomposed by an electric current, when the melted sodium is set free at the cathode and caustic soda is produced at the anode.

Electric Furnace Smelting and Refining.—The

electric furnace has been found very useful for smelting various ores and refining different metals. A furnace for smelting tin ores is constructed in two parts so that they can be bolted together or taken apart. Further, it is provided with trunnions like a gun so that it can be turned a quarter way round. This allows the furnace to stand with the outlet on top when the ore is being smelted, and to turn over so that the tin will run out when it is on its side. Two large graphite electrodes are set in either side of the furnace and these are connected with a dynamo which generates the current.

In making high-grade steel from low-grade steel the electric furnace has proved of great value. The best known furnace for this purpose is the one invented by Herault, of France. The furnace is built up of a steel shell lined with fire-brick, and this is further lined with a thick layer of *dolomite*, that is a mineral which is formed chiefly of *calcium carbonate* and *magnesium carbonate* and of which mountains are made, especially the Swiss Alps. This type is useful because the highest temperatures have little or no effect on it.

Into this bowl-like shell is placed the low-grade steel that is to be refined, when the top, or roof, which is lined with fire-clay, is set on it and the current switched on to the graphite electrodes. Now as low-grade steel contains sulphur and phosphorus and it is these elements that make it brittle, they are made to combine with the bases, magnesia and lime, contained in the dolomite forming the slag under the great heat of the arc, which leaves the steel in a very pure state. The slag, which is then rich in phosphorus, can be used for making fertilizer.

CHAPTER XVIII

SYNTHETIC DIAMONDS AND OTHER GEMS

LONG before chemistry as we know it to-day was born there were men who melted lead and sulphur together and mixed them with salt and mercury in the forlorn hope that from out of the mass would come the yellow metal gold. These old experimenters were called *alchemists*, and while they did not discover the art of transmuting the baser metals into gold, the things they did find out finally led to modern chemistry, and this is worth more to the human race than all the precious metals that have been or ever will be taken from the earth or made by the future arts of man. The alchemists, then, did not live in vain.

For many years after chemistry became a science those who practiced it confined their efforts almost wholly to breaking down substances and learning the elements of which they were formed—that is, they spent much of their time in *analyzing* them. In this way they came to know what elements the various mineral, plant and animal substances were made of and, further, the number of atoms of each element that makes up a molecule of each substance. But as for taking certain elements and making their atoms combine in the right proportion to form old or new substances—well, this savored altogether too much of the tactics of the ancient alchemist.

Hence it is only within the last quarter of a century that chemists have worked toward the end of making atoms of various elements combine as they wished them to, so that they would form substances that Nature has produced or perhaps substances such as she never made. And why does the chemist want to perform these modern miracles? The answer is so that we can have a purer supply, a more plentiful supply or a cheaper supply of a substance that is either scarce, impure or costly, or for all of these reasons put together. The making of different substances by combining the required number of atoms of various elements is called *synthetic chemistry*.

What Diamonds Are Made Of.—Long ago chemists learned that *diamonds* are formed of perfectly pure carbon which had been crystallized by heat and pressure. In making experiments with carbon, which is an element, they found that graphite could be made out of charcoal, that common coal could be changed into gas-carbon, and the diamond converted into coke. They further found that all of these forms of carbon unite with exactly the same quantity of oxygen when they are heated in the open air and, finally, that each of the kinds of carbon could be changed into charcoal.

Now carbon, you will remember, is one of the most

plentiful elements in the earth's crust, but diamond, the crystallized kind, is one of the rarest of substances. Again, each of the three kinds of carbon has properties and characteristics all its own. Graphite is soft to the touch and crystallized; charcoal and other carbon forms are more or less hard and opaque, while the diamond is the hardest of all known substances and transparent. Diamonds are mined chiefly in Brazil, South Africa and Borneo, while a few of them have been found in Georgia and North Carolina.

Wherever they are found they are covered with a dense, brown-colored crust, like the shell of a hazelnut, which looks very much like a pebble. To get out the diamond you have to break the crust just as you have to crack the shell of a nut to get out the kernel. The diamond itself is generally round and transparent and most of them are slightly colored, usually a yellowish tint, though some of them are a bluish-white, while others are brown and black. Occasionally one is found that is perfectly clear and colorless and without a flaw. Such a stone is called a diamond of the *first water* because it looks very much like a drop of the purest water.

Before a diamond will show off its beauty to the best advantage it must be *cut*, that is *facets* must be ground on it, and this is done with *diamond dust*; this is made from diamonds that are either too small or large ones that are too full of flaws to be sold as gems. To cut a diamond it must be set in a bit of lead which, in turn, is fixed to the end of a stick, when the diamond is held down on the surface of a rotating disk, the latter being covered with diamond dust mixed with oil. When the diamond is cut it has numerous flat surfaces, called *facets*, on it, and these *refract* the light in such a way that it flashes forth brilliantly and with a great variety of colors.

Making Diamonds in the Electric Furnace.—Modern chemists have tried just as hard to make diamonds as ever the alchemist worked to make gold out of lead and they have succeeded just a shade better. Though diamonds are formed of carbon in the pure state, no process has yet been found by which they could be made large enough to have any commercial value as an abrasive much less as an ornament. As long as half a century ago when the electric battery was new, chemists sometimes found diamonds in various carbon compounds through which they had passed an electric current, but they were so small that a microscope was necessary to see them.

The first attempt to produce diamonds in an electric furnace since the invention of the dynamo was made by Henri Moissan, a French chemist, in 1894. He examined very carefully into the scheme that Nature employed in making her diamonds, and found that she did so by heating carbon to a very high temperature and letting it cool under an enormous pressure. So Moissan built a small electric furnace the shell of which was of iron, and into this he set a block of *carbonate of lime* on which high temperatures have small effect. In the middle of the block of lime he made a hole just large enough to hold a small graphite crucible. The graphite electrodes, which were an inch in diameter and twelve inches long, rested on top of the block of lime so that when the current was switched on, the arc would form directly over the mouth of the crucible; a cover made of a slab of lime was placed on top of the furnace and this completed the equipment.

He next made a mixture of a small amount of powdered Swedish iron, which is the purest obtainable, and an equal amount of powdered charcoal, made from sugar to insure its being pure. This charge he put into the crucible which in turn he set in the furnace. Then he switched on the electric current and started the arc. The latter took a thousand *amperes* (quantity of electricity) at five hundred *volts* (pressure of electricity). Thus the power used by the arc was equal to about six hundred and seventy horse-power, and this heated the charge in the crucible to about 6,000 degrees Centigrade.

This tremendous heat soon melted the iron and brought it to a highly fluid state with the carbon melted in it. To put the carbon under pressure and make it crystallize into diamonds, the molten mass was suddenly dropped into cold water. As the iron solidified on the outside first, that on the inside expanded against it and exerted a mighty pressure on the carbon, when it became in very truth real diamonds.

The next thing to do was to get the diamonds out of the iron, and this was done by dissolving the latter away with *hydrochloric acid*. This left a rough carbon coating around the diamonds which was removed with *aqua regia*, that is a mixture of nitric and hydrochloric acid. The diamonds thus made were barely large enough to be seen with the naked eye, but they were real though they were not commercially valuable either as an abrasive or for ornaments. Making diamonds of any considerable size is as yet an outstanding achievement of the chemist, for it not only requires an exceedingly high temperature to liquefy the carbon but a tremendous pressure to make it crystallize. It is, however, only a question of time until diamonds as pure and as large as those found in the Kimberley mines will be made *synthetically* and then everybody can wear them if they want to.

Making Synthetic Emeralds.—Besides diamonds the only other really precious stones are the emerald, ruby and sapphire, and all of these are noted for their hardness, beauty of color and brilliancy. Now there is a mineral called *beryl* and the emerald is a very pure variety of it. This gem has a beautiful green color and it was worn by the ancients, who could afford them, not only as an ornament but because they were believed to prevent and cure diseases. It is a matter of history that Emperor Nero wore an eyeglass made of an emerald so that he might see distant objects the better.

Since perfect emeralds are seldom made by Nature those without a flaw are just as costly as diamonds of the same quality, hence making them synthetically appeals to the chemist as much as making diamonds. From a technical point the process seems easier of solution, for high temperatures are not needed, but those that have been made in the laboratory are so small that they have no value. To begin with, the emerald is a *silicate*, that is it is formed of *aluminum silicate*, which in turn is a compound made up of *aluminum, silicon,* and *glucinum*. Aluminum, as you know, is a metal, and silicon and glucinum are elements of the order of carbon and boron, while the brilliant green color of the gem is due to the *chromium* in it.

As the emerald is composed of very different substances from that of the diamond, a process different from that used in making the latter was needed to produce it. Two chemists, Haute-Feuille and Perry, got up a process in 1890 for making synthetic emeralds which consisted first of preparing a solution of *lithium dimolybdate*. Lithium is a very light silver-white metal, like sodium and potassium, while dimolybdate is a yellowish powder made by heating *molybdenite*, which is a sulphide of the metal *molybdenum*.

Next they dissolved aluminum silicate and glucinum silicate, in the exact amounts in which these compounds are found in natural emeralds, in lithium dimolybdate and then added a trace of *chromium oxide*, which is made from the metal *chromium*, to give the gems their green color. This solution was then heated to 400 degrees Centigrade and kept at this temperature continuously for two weeks, when beautiful little emeralds crystallized out of it.

When emeralds can be made large enough to compete with those that are now obtained from Mother Earth it will also be possible to produce *aquamarines* in the same way, for both kinds of stones are formed of the same basic silicates and the only difference between them is that the former are green in color, while the latter have a blue, or bluish-green, color.

SYNTHETIC DIAMONDS AND OTHER GEMS

Making Rubies and Sapphires in the Oxy-Hydrogen Furnace.—We now come to a class of gems that are just as costly and equally as highly prized as diamonds and emeralds, and these are rubies and sapphires. And the interesting part of it is that the last-named gems are made on a commercial scale and are just as large, perfect and beautiful as the finest of the natural stones.

In the preceding chapter we discussed *carborundum*, how it is made in the electric furnace and used instead of *emery* for grinding and polishing metals. Emery is a natural product and is a granular variety of a mineral called *corundum*, which, in turn, is formed of aluminum oxide, the hardest substance known next to the diamond. Now it happens that *aluminum oxide* is also the chief substance of which the ruby and sapphire are composed. Emery is crystallized aluminum oxide with impurities in it, while the ruby and sapphire are crystallized aluminum oxide which, except for the trace of coloring matter in them, are absolutely pure. It does not take nearly as great a heat to crystallize aluminum oxide as it does to crystallize carbon, so instead of an electric furnace, which is employed in making diamonds, an oxy-hydrogen furnace is used for making rubies and sapphires.

How an Oxy-Hydrogen Blowpipe is Made.—An oxy-hydrogen blowpipe is an apparatus so constructed that a flame of hydrogen burns in a blast of oxygen. This type of blowpipe was invented by Dr. Robert Hare, of Philadelphia, who made and used the first one in 1801, and with it he melted *strontium*, a metal that is very much like calcium, and vaporized *platinum*, which has quite a high melting point. When hydrogen and oxygen are mixed (not combined) they are very explosive, and so, in order to burn hydrogen in oxygen the gases must not be allowed to mix until they reach the jet where the flame takes place.

To do this a special jet is needed. In its simplest form the jet consists of a small tube through which the hydrogen flows under pressure and a tube surrounding it through which oxygen is forced under pressure. These gases are compressed in separate steel cylinders and they are connected to their respective hydrogen and oxygen inlets of the jet with rubber tubing. The hydrogen is allowed to flow through the jet first when it is lighted and then the oxygen is turned on, when a solid and almost colorless flame is produced whose temperature is about 6,800 degrees Fahrenheit. At this temperature a watch-spring will burn and scintillate like fireworks, and platinum, one of the most difficult metals to melt, is easily brought to the liquid state.

Now when an oxy-hydrogen flame is directed upon some substance which will neither burn nor melt, the spot where the flame strikes will be so intensely heated that it will give forth a dazzling white light. Such a substance is quicklime, that is *calcium oxide*, and as this is used for the purpose the light is called the *lime light*, or *calcium light*. This light was first produced by Drummond and in the early days it was commonly spoken of as the *Drummond light*. Before the electric arc light came into general use a lime light set in front of a reflector was used as a *spot-light* for stage illumination,

SYNTHETIC DIAMONDS AND OTHER GEMS

and in stereopticons for projecting pictures on a screen.

Another useful apparatus for many purposes is the *oxy-acetylene blowpipe*. You will recall in the preceding chapter on *Electric Furnace Products* that when calcium oxide is heated with carbon in an electric furnace *calcium carbide* is formed, and, further, you will remember that in the chapter on *Good and Bad Gases* we explained that when water came in contact with calcium carbide the reaction set free *acetylene gas*. Now when acetylene gas is used instead of hydrogen in the blowpipe and is burned in a jet of oxygen it makes a flame which is a thousand degrees hotter (about 7,900 degrees Fahrenheit) than that produced by the oxy-hydrogen blowpipe. The *oxy-acetylene torch* as it is called is used for cutting steel, and it is especially useful where buildings with steel girders and columns are to be razed. An oxy-acetylene flame will cut in two a piece of steel an inch thick at the rate of nearly a foot a minute.

How the Oxy-Hydrogen Furnace is Made.—Now we will get back to the making of rubies and sapphires. It seems strange that although aluminum oxide was melted with the oxy-hydrogen blowpipe early in the nineteenth century, it was nearly a hundred years later before anyone thought it worth while to examine the *inside* of the mass that was so formed. When this was finally done it was found that a true crystal was the result and an analysis of it showed that it possessed the same properties as the ruby and sapphire. Then several more years elapsed before M. Verneuil, of France, invented the oxy-hydrogen furnace in which the aluminum oxide falls through the flame of the blowpipe in a continuous stream.

The Verneuil furnace consists of a base on which there is mounted a stand having a screw adjustment so that the latter can be raised or lowered. On the stand is an earthenware rod about the size of a candle and which has a tapering top like the point of a lead pencil. Over the stand and rod sets the furnace chamber and this is supported by an upright rod fixed to the base. In the top of this rests the jet of the blowpipe, while the other end supports a funnel-shaped box in which there is a sieve that holds the aluminum oxide.

The lower end of the box is connected to a thin metal tube which has an inlet in its upper end for admitting the hydrogen, and the jet is at its lower end. Surrounding the hydrogen tube, through which the aluminum oxide falls, is a second tube that has an inlet at the top for admitting the oxygen and an outlet at the bottom so that the hydrogen flame can burn in it. When the blowpipe is lighted, the point of the flame strikes directly on the end of the earthenware rod. Finally a tapping device, made like an electric bell with the gong removed, is secured to the top of the support rod and this is connected with and operated by a battery. With this furnace rubies and sapphires have been satisfactorily produced.

How Synthetic Rubies and Sapphires Are Made.—As both rubies and sapphires are formed of aluminum oxide the method of making them is exactly the same.

SYNTHETIC DIAMONDS AND OTHER GEMS

The finest rubies are those that have a *pigeon-blood color* and when these are pure and weigh two carats, or more, they are often worth ten times as much as a white diamond of the same quality. To make a ruby of a pigeon-blood color you put into the sieve in the box at the top of the furnace some *aluminum oxide* with a trace of *chromium oxide*, which is a green powder and yet which, strange to relate, gives the gem its red color.

This done, light the oxy-hydrogen jet and set the electric tapper into operation when a fine stream of the charge will begin to fall through the inner tube; on reaching the jet it passes through it and the flame, when it melts and drops onto the end of the earthenware rod, where it builds up a little pear-shaped mass, or *boulé* (pronounced *boul-a*) as it is called. This *boulé* is a crystallized mass and it is as genuine and, when cut, as beautiful as any ruby that was ever mined in far-famed Burma.

Synthetic sapphires are made in exactly the same way as are rubies, except a trace of *titanium oxide* is mixed with the aluminum oxide to give the gem its characteristic blue color. Gems of other colors, the like of which no mortal eye ever beheld until Verneuil brought forth his process, can be as easily made by using other metallic salts to color them with, or, still more wonderful, a perfectly colorless sapphire, called a *white sapphire*, can be produced.

Not the least remarkable thing about making these gems in the oxy-hydrogen furnace is that it takes only half an hour to make a *boulé* weighing thirty carats, and from this two stones can be cut each of which weighs six carats. Further, one operator can take care of ten, or more, furnaces, so both the labor as well as the raw material is cheap. You can get a fair idea of the extent of the synthetic gem industry when I tell you that six million carats of sapphires and ten million carats of rubies are produced every year. But these gems, however pure and beautiful, do not fetch the fancy prices that oriental stones do; instead, the prices range anywhere from a quarter to five dollars a carat, which brings them within reach of everybody.

CHAPTER XIX

RADIUM, THE MODERN MARVEL

WHAT would you think of a fuel that you could put in a stove and which, without burning, would give off enough heat to cook not only one meal but a thousand meals, and then be of exactly the same size that it was at the beginning? Well, we must admit that this is not yet possible, though it is not that we haven't such a fuel, but because we can't get hold of enough of it at one time. The fuel is called *radium*.

Shortly after radium was discovered by M. and Mme. Curie it was found that a bit of it gave off enough heat to raise an equal weight of water from the freezing state to the boiling point in one hour, and it has been said that the heat developed by ten pounds of radium would keep up enough steam to run a one horse-power engine, if not forever, then nearly so. But there isn't a pound of pure radium in the world; in fact, there hasn't been more than an ounce of it extracted since it was discovered; and even if there was it could not be used for fuel, for it is at once too costly and too dangerous.

How Radium Was Discovered.—Now let us find

out just what this wonderful element is and how it was discovered. It is almost thirty years since Professor Roentgen, of Germany, discovered the *X-rays*—those curious rays which pass through wood, leather and flesh but are stopped by metals, bone and other dense substances. These rays affect a photographic plate like light waves for they are waves exactly like light but so short they cannot be seen by the eye.

Almost as soon as the X-rays were discovered scientists everywhere began to test phosphorescent bodies, rare earths and minerals in order to find out if any of these substances would give out waves of a like nature. About a year after the X-rays were discovered, Professor Becquerel, of Paris, found that certain salts of *uranium*, a metal which occurs in nature chiefly in the mineral known as *pitchblend*, or *uraninite*, emitted, that is gave out, waves which passed through paper and some other opaque substances, were stopped by metals and would affect a photographic plate. These radiations were called *Becquerel rays*.

Two years later, that is in 1898, Professor Schmidt and Madame Curie, of Paris, found that the salts of *thorium*, an element that occurs principally in the mineral *thorite*, emitted rays exactly like those of uranium, and then M. and Mme. Curie made an investigation of a large number of the metals, rare earths, minerals, elements and compounds, when they discovered that *pitchblend*, in which uranium is found, gave off rays which are far more active, that is powerful, than uranium alone. The Curies were convinced that there was some other element in pitchblend which produced these very active rays and they began a long series of chemical operations that finally resulted in the separation from it of two radio-active elements; the first of these, which is a thousand times more active than uranium, they named *radium*, and the second, which was less active, they called *polonium*, after Poland where Mme. Curie was born. Then, in 1899, M. Debierne discovered another radio-active element in pitchblend and this he named *actinium*.

How Radium is Extracted.—But radium claimed the greatest attention for it was far more active than either polonium or actinium. As there is only about one-sixth of an ounce of radium salts in a ton of pitchblend it is no small labor to extract it. To do this, the uranium that is in the pitchblend is separated from it first and the

THE MANUFACTURE OF RADIUM

Five hundred tons of ore, and five thousand different operations are required to make one gram (thimbleful) of radium.

pitchblend is then successively treated with hot caustic soda, hydrochloric acid and hot sodium carbonate, that is sal soda. The solid matter which now remains contains *radium carbonate* mixed with *barium carbonate* and there is also some lead, calcium, polonium and actinium in it. These latter elements are now removed by further chemical operations, when *radium chloride* and *barium chloride* alone remain. As the barium chloride dissolves more easily than the radium, it is crystallized out, when only radium chloride remains.

But radium chloride is a salt of radium and it was not until several years later that Mme. Curie was able to separate the radium from its chloride. The way she did this was by using the *electrolysis process;* the cathode was formed of *mercury* and the anode of *platinum-iridium*, while the solution was made of radium chloride. When the current was made to pass through the solution it was *electrolyzed* and the pure metallic radium was deposited on the cathode when it formed an amalgam with the mercury. The cathode was then heated in an iron crucible in an electric furnace, with a current of pure hydrogen flowing over it. When the heat had driven off all the mercury there remained in the crucible a minute bit of brilliant white metal which was pure radium.

Some Properties of Radium.—Radium, that is the pure metal, has the color and lustre of silver and while it does not tarnish when it is not exposed to air, the moment the air touches it, the bright metallic lustre disappears. When a bit of radium is thrown into water it rapidly decomposes it. Not only do the rays of radium pass through certain opaque substances and act on photographic plates, but they give off light and heat continuously. It was Mme. Curie and M. Laborde who discovered that radium is always just a little warmer than the temperature of the air around it, which means that radium is constantly giving out heat. This was learned when these chemists had obtained their first sample of pure radium; a particle of it dropped on a sheet of paper and it not only blackened it but it carbonized it as well.

Radium is seldom used in its pure state but generally as a salt and this is usually sealed in a little glass tube. In this condition it looks just like so much common salt, but if you take it into the dark you will see that it is luminous like phosphorus. Another of its remarkable properties is that of making other compounds luminous when it is held close to or is mixed with them. Thus if the radium is held close to a diamond the latter will glow with a soft radiance; again, if it is brought near *zinc sulphide* this compound will glow with a bright phosphorescence; if you were to examine the zinc sulphide when it is acted on by a particle of radium with a microscope of low power, you would see that the light is set up by little flashes, and the closer the radium is held to the zinc sulphide the brighter the flashes become. This curious action was discovered by Sir William Crookes, who constructed a little instrument called the *spinthariscope* for showing the flashes to the best advantage.

Uses of Luminous Material.—It takes only the smallest imaginable particle of radium to make a considerable quantity of zinc sulphide luminous when they are mixed together. This is the substance which is now so largely used for making the faces of watches luminous, and its use is being widely extended by painting danger points of machinery, gasoline gauges and other parts of automobiles, electric switches, fire alarms, safe combinations and other objects with the radium material.

How to Tell Radio-Active Substances.—Another strange property of radium is that its rays make air a good conductor of static electricity, and so if it is brought close to an electrified body the latter will immediately lose its charge. Now there is a simple little instrument called the *gold leaf electroscope*, which consists of a couple of strips of gold leaf, about an inch long, one of the ends of each one being attached to one end of a brass rod. The free end of the rod is slipped through a piece of hard rubber, the end of the rod with the gold leaves on it is placed into a wide-necked glass bottle, and the rubber is set into the neck like a cork.

When the gold leaves of the electroscope are charged with electricity by means of a static machine, the leaves, since they are both charged to the same sign, will diverge, that is fly apart, at their free ends and they will remain so until the electricity that is on them leaks away through the rod into the air. If the air is perfectly dry they will remain charged for a long time, but if the air is moist the charge will soon pass into it, for dry air is a non-conductor and moist air is a conductor of electricity.

When, however, a bit of radium, or radium salts,

or any other compound that is radio-active, is held closely to the brass rod that projects into the air of a charged electroscope, the air is instantly *ionized*, that is made conducting, the leaves of the electroscope are quickly discharged and collapse. The electroscope, then, provides an easy way to tell whether or not a substance is radio-active and the extent of its activity.

Action of Radium on the Human Body.—Very shortly after the discovery of radium it was found that if a bit of it was placed close to any part of the human body, it would burn it in very much the same way as the X-rays. Further experiments with larger quantities of it showed that it produced very bad sores and ulcers and that it was next to impossible to heal them. On the other hand, when properly applied it has a decided healing effect on cancers and other malignant growths, and to-day radium is best known for its curative properties and nearly every hospital has its own little tube of radium salts.

Kinds of Radium Rays.—The action of radium salts on a photographic plate, when they generate heat, produce phosphorescence, ionize the air, and cause sores and heal them, is due to the rays that are given off by them. Now it has been found that the rays are made up of three different kinds and these are known as *alpha* rays, *beta* rays, and *gamma* rays.

These different rays were separated by Professor Rutherford, who inserted a bit of radium chloride, or other radium salt, in the hollow of a cup-shaped piece of lead which rested on a level surface and then placed a magnet at right angles to it. The magnet bent the alpha-rays out of the straight path, and bent the beta-rays over like the alpha-rays, only more so and in the opposite direction, while the gamma-rays shot up and out from it in a straight line.

Alpha-rays are made up of atoms of *helium* gas and each of them carry a charge of positive electricity. These atoms travel at a rate of about twenty thousand miles per second, or a little more than one-tenth as fast as light. The heat generated by radium is caused by the collisions of the atoms of the α-rays with themselves and when they strike a substance like zinc sulphide they make it luminous. Beta-rays are, in turn, very small particles of matter that always carry a charge of negative electricity; these rays are turned so far out of their natural course that they will strike against and affect a photographic plate that is placed under the lead cup which contains the radium. They have a speed of about one hundred thousand miles a second, or a little more than half of that of light.

The magnet has no effect on the gamma-waves and in this respect they are very much like X-rays but their power to pass through substances is much greater than the latter. These rays are believed to be due to the action of beta-rays that are set up inside of it and which strike the salt of which it forms a part. In using radium salts for experimental and other purposes no attempt is made to separate the three different kinds of rays, but they are all used together to produce the desired effect.

What Happens to Radium.—Before the discovery of radium we were taught that all of the elements had existed ever since the beginning of the universe, that they could not be changed in any way, and that they would continue to exist to the end of time. Now radium is an element but it was not always radium and it is slowly but surely changing into other elements. So we are back to the belief of the old alchemists that one element may be changed into an entirely different one, and so the hope has been revived that the baser metals, or their equivalents, may be transmuted into gold.

Not only is it known that the ancestor of radium is uranium, and that radium is slowly changing into other elements the end-product of which is lead, but that the metal potassium is radio-active to a slight extent; this shows, according to Professor Martin, of London, that all the other elements are changing into still other elements, though the rate of change is so slow that no way has yet been found actually to prove it. Fortunately radium changes into other elements fast enough so that it is possible to show just what is going on.

As just stated, radium was not always radium but in the beginning was uranium, which is the heaviest of all known elements. *Uranium* changed first into *uranium X1*, this into *uranium X2*, this into *uranium 2*, this into *ionium*, and it is this element that changes into *radium*. Next when *radium* splits up it changes into *helium*, and *niton*; helium, as explained before, is made up of alpha-rays; and niton is the emanation of radium after the other part of the latter has changed into helium. *Niton*, then, changes into *radium A*, this into *radium B*, this into *radium C*, this into *radium D*, this into *radium E*, this into *radium F*, which resembles the metal bismuth, this into *polonium*, and finally polonium changes into *lead*. The curious thing about the lead which is evolved through the above list of elements is that it is exactly like ordinary lead in all respects except it is not quite so heavy. In this way then does the transmutation of lead from uranium take place.

The transmutation of uranium into radium and this element into lead is a perfectly natural process; but Dr. Rutherford, of England, who has done the major part of the recent research work in the field of radio-activity, has been able to cause the transmutation of various other elements artificially; this, however, does not at all mean that it is now possible to transmute lead, or other metals, into gold, that is to make gold synthetically, but it does point the way by which it may sometime be done.

The Crookes' Spinthariscope.—The word spinthariscope comes from two Greek words which mean *spark* and *to see* and this was the name Sir William Crookes gave to a little instrument which he invented so that the constant bombardment of the radium atoms against a target of zinc sulphide could be seen to the best advantage. It consists of a tube, about three-fourths of an inch in diameter and two inches long, with a zinc sulphide screen in one end, and a point covered with radium salts supported by a wire one-fourth of an inch in front of the center.

In the other end of the tube is fixed a magnifying

lens. Now on looking through the lens you will see minute bright streaks shoot out in all directions like a swarm of meteors in a November sky. These streaks of light are caused by the breaking of the crystals of zinc sulphide whenever one of the helium atoms strikes it. You can see the same thing if you will rub together two pieces of lump sugar in the dark.

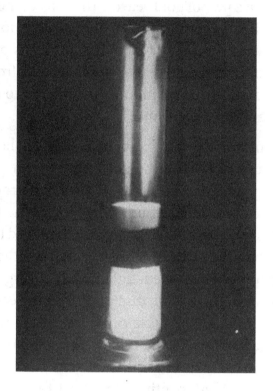

THE WORLD'S SUPPLY OF RADIUM

Now manufactured commercially but in inconceivably small quantities. The white (lower) section is the total amount made by the Standard Chemical Company (72 grams). The black (middle) is the total estimated amount produced by other American companies (40 grams). The gray (upper) section is the estimated amount refined in Europe.

The Strutt Radium Clock—The Strutt Radium "Clock" is a curious apparatus devised by R. J. Strutt, of London, in which the leaves of an electroscope are charged by radium and discharged into the earth automatically so that they diverge and collapse with clock-like regularity. The apparatus consists of a tube of radium salt whose lower end is fixed to one end of each one of a pair of gold-leaves. This part of the device is sealed in a larger glass tube whose lower portion is covered with tin-foil and from this the air is pumped. The tin-foil is connected to a wire that leads from it to the outside of the tube and this is soldered to an iron rod driven into the ground.

The first thing that happens is that the beta-rays of the radium charge the gold leaves with positive electricity and, as like kinds of electricity repel like kinds, they spread apart until they touch the tin-foil; when this takes place their charge is discharged through the wire into the earth and the leaves fall together. Then the radium charges them again, they diverge, make contact with the tin-foil, discharge into the earth and collapse. And so the cycle of operations is repeated and if the vacuum in the tube is perfect enough, the leaves don't wear out, and the earth connection is maintained, it will continue to repeat for a thousand years or more.

CHAPTER XX

THE COMING MIRACLES OF CHEMISTRY

In the dim *pliocene* age, a million years or so ago, when man had just emerged from his unknown ancestors, his intelligence was but a shade higher than that of the anthropoids[23] who lived at the same time. His life then was a simple one for he lived in the country that is now Egypt, or, more likely, in the valley to the north of it and which is now covered with the waters of the Mediterranean Sea. Since the climate was salubrious the year round, even as it is now, he needed no clothes, and the food he ate was at hand for the mere plucking or the killing of it. He was an animal, restless, energetic and curious, and now and then he would get a thought in the back of his brain. His was the simple life, for *work* had not yet been invented.

Man the Non-chemist.—As man passed on and up through the glacial age he learned how to make fire, eat cooked meats, fashion stone implements, use the skins

---

[23] Animals that are something like a man in form and other characteristics.

of animals to cover him, to draw pictures and to live in caves. As he did not have to do real work and as there was nothing his fellow man had that he did not have—except perhaps his neighbor's daughter—he too lived a simple and unintelligent life. But times were changing, and following came the nimble-witted man, or *homo-sapiens* as he is called, and his ability to observe and to think was far greater than any of his ancestors. He it was who discovered the wheel, how to grow things for food, to tan leather, to weave cloth and to make pottery. But the crowning discovery of his time was a heavy, reddish substance which fire would not burn, water would not change, and which he could hammer into various shapes without breaking. It was as wonderful to him as radium is to us, but we now consider it very commonplace for it was the metal *copper*. Primitive man set out to find more of it and having found it he wrought it into ornaments and implements. A new age was upon the human race and they progressed, for it was the age of copper, a little higher intelligence and of *work*.

Man the Alchemist.—Then one by one other metals were found, including gold and lead and mercury, and things that were non-metals, as salt and sulphur. Imagine the interest that mercury, the liquid metal, must have caused when it was discovered, and sulphur, which burns with a ghastly light, gives off stifling fumes, which when melted changes into a molasses-like liquid and when cooled in water stretches like rubber! By the time the human race had reached this advanced stage of progress there were many things a few of its members had and which all of them wanted, but because *gold* was the scarcest and the hardest to get it was the chief object of their desire.

The observers, who lived only a few hundred years ago, had examined four other things in nature, namely, *earth, air, fire,* and *water,* and these they called *the elements*[24] and they thought they could make any substance they wanted to by merely combining them; thus they believed that sulphur was made by fire acting on air; mercury by air acting on water, and salt by water acting on earth. Their big idea, though, was that by compounding the above so-called elements they could obtain the *essence,* and having once got that they needed only to add it to lead to change the latter into gold.

Very quickly indeed did this alluring belief find favor, and soon many men were working in secret laboratories melting metals, boiling solutions, mixing solids and performing all sorts of experiments without knowing what they were doing but with the full knowledge of what they wanted to get, and this was the coveted *essence.* Each alchemist had his own formula for transmuting lead into gold and one of these was to *calcine* it, that is to burn it, and by adding some of the wonderful *essence* to it, the baser metal would change into the finer one at once.

That this was possible was to their simple minds an assured fact, for when a large mass of lead was fired in a furnace, a bead of silver was always found in the

---

[24]So called by the alchemists because they were believed to be the fundamentals of which everything else was made.

charred remains. We know now that all native lead, that is pure lead as it is found in nature, has a small amount of silver mixed with it and that this was separated out by the burning process. Had they known this too, it would have only confirmed the idea already fixed in their minds that the lead was growing into silver. It is clear that man had mentally improved, though not greatly, over his prehistoric ancestors but the age in which he lived had taken on a much more complex aspect.

As time moved on apace, the latter-day alchemists did some very good work for they were *thinking* about the substances they were working with as well as of transmuting lead into gold, and *thought* is the only *essence* that has got, or will ever get, the human race anywhere. One of these thinking alchemists was Von Hohenheim, a Swiss doctor who was born in the memorable year of 1492, and who called himself Paracelsus. He discovered the way to make *laudanum* and so benefited medicine; and he was also the first to make hydrogen which was a real experiment in chemistry.

Man the Chemist.—From this first step more than two hundred years passed before the next one was taken, and this was when Robert Boyle, of England, studied the air and explained how and why things burned in it. It was Boyle, too, who showed how foolish the alchemists' idea was of the *four elements* and explained just what an *element* consisted of, namely a substance that cannot be decomposed into any simpler substance. After Boyle, came Jean Ray, of France, who proved that air was not a chemical compound but a mechanical mixture of two gases, though he did not know what these gases were. Later on Joseph Priestley, of England, made one of the gases of the air which was oxygen and Lavoisier, the French chemist, found that the other gas was nitrogen. It was Lavoisier who classified the acids, bases and salts, and his system is still in use. These were the first real chemists.

The discovery of the *voltaic pile*, an electro-chemical apparatus for generating a current of electricity, and out of which grew the electric battery, was made by Volta, an Italian scientist, in 1798; Sir Humphry Davy, of London, decomposed water by means of it in 1800, and shortly after he obtained the new metals, *sodium* and *potassium*, by the same means. Then in 1808 John Dalton, of England, got up the *atomic theory* which states that an atom is an exceedingly minute particle of matter, that each element is formed of atoms having exactly the same weight, and that an atom cannot be divided by any known means. It is easy to get the idea of Dalton's atom for all you have to do is to think of it as a little sugar-coated pill.

Faraday's researches on the action of electric currents and magnetism in 1801 led to the invention of the *induction coil*, or spark coil, which Ruhmkorff brought to a high state of perfection in 1846 and, finally, about 1850, Geissler produced a new air pump and pumped out glass tubes which he had previously filled with gases of various kinds. A pair of wires were sealed in the ends of the tubes and these he connected with the induction coil. When the high tension current passed through these *Geissler tubes*, as they came to be called, they gave forth a soft glowing light of various colors according to the gas they contained.

The subject of the electric discharge in gases was thoroughly investigated by Sir William Crookes in 1879. With an air pump of special construction he was able to exhaust glass tubes to a much higher degree than had ever been obtained before, so that the number of molecules of gas remaining in the tubes were very few and far between. When these were acted upon by the high tension current, new phenomena were produced and Crookes announced he had discovered a *fourth state of matter*, that it was neither solid, liquid nor gaseous, and this he called *radiant matter*. And he was right, for the particles which are thrown off from the cathode of a *high vacuum tube*, or *Crookes* tube as it is called, are *cathode rays*, that is rays made up of *electrons*, which are in turn particles of negative electricity each of which is much smaller than an atom.

These cathode rays, or streams of electrons, move with a velocity very much higher than a projectile fired from a gun and tend to travel in straight lines. In experimenting with a tube, in one end of which he had placed a thin sheet of aluminium, Lenard found, in 1894, that the electrons of the cathode rays passed through it, and then, Roentgen, the next year, discovered the *X-rays*.

In the beginning of the same year, 1895, an important discovery was made by Lord Rayleigh and Sir William Ramsay; this was a new gas that is in the air, and to it they gave the name of *argon;* then a few months later Ramsay discovered another new gas which was very like argon but which he obtained by boiling a mineral called *clévite* with dilute sulphuric acid; this gas he called *helium*, because the same gas had been discovered by Janssen and Lockyer in the sun more than a quarter of a century before; they named the gas *helium* which is the Greek word for *sun*, and these two gases were shown to be the same by means of the *spectroscope*. Now clévite contains *uranium* and the fact that it gives off helium connects it up with radio-activity. Finally, Ramsay discovered two more new gases which he called *krypton* and *xenon*, and the way he did this was to liquefy a large amount of argon and let it evaporate, when the two new gases remained behind because they were the heavier.

In the preceding chapter we discussed other things such as the discovery of the Becquerel rays and of radium, as well as the work of Becquerel, Curie, Rutherford and other great chemists. And you have already seen that instead of the atom being indivisible it is really made up of particles of positive electricity around which surge electrons, or particles of negative charges of electricity, just as the planets revolve around the sun. You have also seen that these electrons fly off from the atom and some of them, when they are emitted from radium as α-rays, become helium. But the most wonderful thing of all is the transmutation of uranium into radium and radium into lead.

Now hydrogen is the lightest element known, having an atomic weight of 1, while uranium is the heaviest element that has been discovered and has an atomic weight of 238; this changes into radium whose atomic weight is 226, and this changes into niton, or radium emanation, whose atomic weight is 224; niton further changes into bismuth whose atomic weight is 208; and, finally, this changes into lead whose atomic weight is 207. This is as far as the natural transmutation goes, but if a further change could be made, the lead would change into thallium whose atomic weight is 204, this finally into mercury whose atomic weight is 200 and this into gold whose atomic weight is 197. The following table places the atomic weights of these elements more clearly before your eye, and you can easily see at a glance the general stages of uranium as it passes into lead and, also, that but three more transmutations are needed to change the lead into gold.

Table of Transmutations

Uranium into Lead		Lead into Gold	
Element	Atomic Weight	Element	Atomic Weight
Uranium	238	Lead	207
Radium	226	Thallium	204
Niton	224	Mercury	200
Bismuth	208	Gold	197
Lead	207		

That the transmutation of the elements can be accomplished by the chemist as well as by nature has recently been proved by Rutherford who bombarded nitrogen gas with the α-*rays* of radium, which are atoms of helium. When the helium atoms strike the nitrogen atoms something happens that is very much like two locomotives running toward each other at high speed on a single track and which meet head-on; that is to say, the nitrogen atom explodes and the pieces form new atoms which are atoms of hydrogen and helium.

Not only has Rutherford broken up the nitrogen atom but he has done the same thing with the atoms of oxygen, chlorine, sodium, aluminum and carbon, and these, too, have yielded hydrogen and helium. Here, then, is the transmutation of elements controlled by man just as certainly as when nature changes radium into lead but it is done on even a more minute scale and so does not at all show how the transmutation of metals on a large scale can be affected; but neither did Faraday's experiment of passing a wire through a magnetic field, and which set up a feeble electric current in it, show how high tension currents of thousands of horse-power, such as we use to-day, could be generated. But it pointed out that a current could be set up, just as Rutherford's experiments point out that the transmutation of the elements is possible. All we need to grow the oak is an acorn and some soil.

As these last pages are written, the newspapers are carrying accounts of synthetic gold being made in Germany, but this is certainly not true for it is far, too far, an advance in the state of the art in much too short a time. Synthetic gold is not a product of the present but it will be of the future. And anyway there are far more important things to be done in the realm of chemistry than making gold and diamonds, and chief among these is the making of synthetic food and the production of cheap and unlimited power.

The energy stored up in the nucleus, or core, of an atom of whatever kind has been believed by scientists for many years to be very great, and it is now known that the atoms of helium which are projected from radium into space set free an enormous amount of energy, probably millions of times greater than that of a like amount of TNT (trinitrotoluene) and billions of times that which is produced by the burning of an equal amount of coal. Our chemists have shown us that we are living in a very intelligent age and a very complex one where *work* is the watchword of the world.

Man the Superchemist.—It used to delight Lord Kelvin to scare us moderns by showing mathematically how soon the coal supply of the world would give out; and what he said was not only true but it is also only a question of time until the water powers give out as well. Where the human race is going to get its power from when these natural sources are gone has occupied the thought of not a few of our greatest scientists. Radiant energy from the sun direct, energy from the tides, from the heat of the interior of the earth, or from the rotation of the earth itself, have all been given consideration. But it is more than probable that by the time other sources of energy are really needed, the superchemist will have unlocked the atom and so will give to man its tremendous power to do the world's work.

In 1898 Sir William Crookes startled the world by declaring that unless the farmers raised far more wheat

THE COMING MIRACLES OF CHEMISTRY

per acre than they had yet done the white races would either have to use other grains or suffer a decrease in population, which means that the oriental races would then forge ahead of us. The way to increase the yield of wheat is by using fertilizers, and every year since he made the statement, except during the World War, more wheat per acre has been raised so that we are, apparently, as far from the end of a wheat famine as we were in 1898. The world gets its phosphates from the United States, its nitrates from Chili, and its potash from Germany, and there are great deposits of all of these fertilizers, but at the present rate they are being used up, there must finally come a time when they will be exhausted. And then what?

While we know of no way to produce potash cheaply either by making it synthetically or otherwise, chemists have learned how to fix the nitrogen of the air by passing an electric spark through it, and this product is being made wherever cheap power can be had and it is being used for fertilizing the soil as well as for many other purposes. And long before the potash and phosphate beds are exhausted, chemists will find a means for making both of them from the elements which are everywhere around us in abundance but which are not at all easy to separate from their mixtures or compounds; and these synthetic fertilizers will keep the wheat fields going for another long time to come. In the meantime the superchemists will be hard at work devising processes for making food in the same direct way, that is by synthesis, as indigo and sapphires are made. This is not a mere fanciful forecast but it is based on what has already been done.

As far back as 1828, Wöhler, a German chemist, built up out of ordinary mineral substances a white, crystalline compound called *urea* which is naturally found in the bodies of animals. It was the first time in the history of chemistry that an *organic* compound, that is living matter, or matter which once lived, was made of *inorganic* substances, or matter which has never lived. As urea contains a large amount of ammonia it is now made in car-load lots. Many other organic compounds have been made from inorganic substances since Wöhler's time.

In 1863 Marcellin Berthelot, of France, made fats and other organic compounds, that is, compounds like those of living matter. This he did by taking various elements found free in nature or in mineral compounds, and building them up little by little, adding an atom of carbon, of hydrogen, of nitrogen or oxygen as it was needed.

In the first few years of this century Emil Fischer, of Germany, made *protein*, or *albumen*, as it is commonly known, that peculiar compound of which the white of egg is made, in the same way that Berthelot built up his compounds, but as it is very complex he had to add atoms of sulphur, phosphorus and iron. It cost Fischer about five hundred dollars in time and money to make half as much albumen as there is in an egg, and as long as Madam Hen and Mr. Beef can produce eggs and meat cheaper than the superchemist they will be allowed to do so. But should they ever go on a strike, or become extinct, butcher shops will become a thing of the dead past and man will buy his fats and proteins at the chemist shops.

And the synthetic product will be better than that of flying birds and hoofed animals that formerly supplied man with a large part of his foodstuffs, for there will be no such things as cold storage to freeze the taste out of them, or diseases to poison them. When this halcyon age arrives, everyone will have all the diamonds and other gems he wants, gold will be more plentiful than lead is now, power will be as cheap as water, and life will be one long, sweet dream. Then will man have become ultra-intelligent, and he will again live the simple life of the pliocene man, for work will have once more lost its meaning.

CPSIA information can be obtained
at www.ICGtesting.com
Printed in the USA
BVHW081433230722
642607BV00002B/234